# A Time to Fish and A Time to Dry Nets

## —Lake of the Woods—

# A Time to Fish and A Time to Dry Nets

## —Lake of the Woods—

### Alvin Johnston

Copyright © 1996 by Alvin Johnston

All rights reserved. No part of this publication may be reproduced in any form or by any means without prior permission of the Publisher or Author, except for brief excerpts in reviews.

Published by Lakewood Publishing Company
Box 907, Warroad, Minnesota 56763

Printed and bound by BookMasters, Inc.
Mansfield, Ohio 44905

Laser printing and the 150 line halftone prints by MacGregor Litho, Inc., Park Falls, Wisconsin 54552

Some of these chapters were orginally published in the *Warroad Pioneer*. "Reeling Them In" was orginally published by the *National Fisherman*.

Photographs are the author's unless otherwise noted.

This book is dedicated to the memory of my brother, Dorrance H. Johnston, who discovered Lake of the Woods' richest resources.

"Never Jump Over A Mud Puddle In Two Jumps"

*Roy R. Duggan*

# A Time to Fish and A Time to Dry Nets

|  | MAP | viii |
|---|---|---|
|  | ACKNOWLEDGEMENTS | ix |
|  | FOREWORD | xi |
| 1 | Fort St. Charles | 1 |
| 2 | Early Days and Fire Days | 8 |
| 3 | Grandpa Guhl—Commercial Fishing | 17 |
| 4 | Dad and Early Warroad Days. | 34 |
| 5 | Diphtheria—Small Pox | 44 |
| 6 | Basketball Was King—Playing Hockey. | 50 |
| 7 | Fish Peddlers and Lamplighters | 56 |
| 8 | First Airplane Ride | 64 |
| 9 | Home Ice Delivery—Billy Booze | 79 |
| 10 | The Mighty Scout | 86 |
| 11 | Winter Commercial Fishing and Slush | 97 |
| 12 | Little Mike's Death—Lake Casualties | 101 |
| 13 | Prohibition—Ma & Pa Teachout | 109 |
| 14 | Chief Makes Chief | 118 |
| 15 | Armistice Day Storm. | 125 |
| 16 | Northwest Angle Logging. | 130 |
| 17 | Warroad Mink Ranching | 138 |
| 18 | Hunting and Icing Down | 145 |
| 19 | Windsledding and Two Gun | 152 |
| 20 | Blue Water | 160 |
| 21 | Fall Freeze-up With D.H. | 172 |
| 22 | Pulling Nets | 183 |
| 23 | Driftwood Point Accident | 189 |
| 24 | Big Moe Fire | 193 |
| 25 | Northwest Angle Closing | 203 |
| 26 | Battle Over Trawling | 224 |
| 27 | Fighting for our Lives | 235 |
| 28 | From Fishing to Gambling Casinos | 243 |
| 29 | Reeling Them In | 251 |

# ACKNOWLEDGEMENTS

There are many who have provided both encouragement and assistance in the writing of this book and I wish I could identify each one.

I thank all of you for your suggestions and/or corrections after reading the manuscript for historical or grammatical errors before it was sent to the printers.

Special thanks to:

Rose Johnson for help with the Indian history;

The Warroad Pioneer and Marvin Window's Technical Publications Department for their assistance with the photographs, and to their photo technician Annie Bendickson;

Spike and Gordie at MacGregor Litho for invaluable printing and photo help.

Ole Swanson for your Warroad Area books—they are invaluable for reference;

My sons Alan and Arthur, my daughter Arlene Lodahl, and my daughter-in-law Nadine;

My grandsons Derrick, Jesse and Gabe; my niece Margaret Marvin;

And Julie Nordine, Pam Peterson, Hal Bakke, and Beth Marvin;

And last, but not least, my wife of fifty-four years, Alberta.

# FOREWORD

I think of Lake of the Woods as home. Not being a bird or a fish, I know it is only a passion of the mind, but it is real to me. Five generations of my family felt the same way.

To the pioneers, "War Path" (Warroad) was not the attraction—it was Lake of the Woods. Working on it, living on it, and sometimes even dying on it was acceptable. It was our source of food, money, and recreation twelve months of the year. Winter and summer. Even when she was mean and angry we admired and loved her. Somehow or other we were never afraid of her. She only presented a challenge to us, never a threat.

Like on all bodies of water, sailing and working on it offers adventure. Lake of the Woods has its share of personalities, some became part of the folklore about the lake. Every word in this book happened, and I have attempted to capture the experiences writing in my own way. I have not had these stories professionally rewritten. The one story not my own is by Arthur Johnston, my son. He was the last commercial fisherman on the Minnesota side of Lake of the Woods. His story of the last day belongs in this book.

I have worked for the past ten years preparing this book, trying to record "the way it was" for the commercial fishermen. My tales will never happen again on Lake of the Woods. The adventure and challenge of working "the big lake" will never be experienced by future generations. Security and well-regulated lives are now what most people experience. My stories are for them. I hope the reader will capture the excitement and thrill of a one-on-one struggle between the lake, the fisherman, and the society.

I hope this book will make a contribution to the memory of the commercial fishermen that harvested the food from Lake of the Woods and while doing so, made Warroad their home.

# 1

## Fort St. Charles

In 1670 King Charles II of England granted the Hudson's Bay Company its charter to search for fur pelts in Canada's Hudson Bay area. They soon penetrated into the Lake of the Woods territory which was controlled by the French adventurers and missionaries.

With its 14,000 islands, Lake of the Woods was a lush wilderness: rich in trees, flowers, birds, mammals, fish and insects. Relatively easy to reach through the Rainy River basin with its hundreds of lakes, Rainy River was to become the important link to reach Lake of the Woods.

Wild rice, fish, moose, caribou and other game of the region, as well as great flocks of migrating or nesting wild fowl, supplied the newcomers with the necessities of life, just as they had supplied the Sioux Indian tribes with their livelihood for hundreds of years.

Lake of the Woods was a great storehouse of luxurious pelts, such as mink, beaver, fox, wolf and muskrat. In the dry, cold climate the underfur be-

## 2   TIME TO FISH—TIME TO DRY NETS

came soft and silky, covered with thick luxuriant guard hair that sparkled and glistened when made into a gorgeous fur coat.

Easy to catch and plentiful, the muskrat was the bread-and-butter pelt to trappers. Somewhat larger in size than a mink, the muskrat made an attractive coat selling for half the price of mink.

Thriving in marshlands, the muskrat was trapped in the Northwest Angle Inlet, Sand Point Bay, Elm Creek and Willow Creek to the mouth of the Warroad River. In the wintertime thousands of muskrat houses dotted every marshland around Lake of the Woods. Each house was six to eight feet in diameter and about three feet high. Made out of lake cane and seaweed, the house was the winter home to a large family of the old and the young.

The muskrats would dive to the bottom of the lake and bring up mouthful of mud to plaster the inside of their house so it would stay warm and not freeze up during the winter months. In the center of each house there was a hole through the ice, large enough to allow them to feed on seaweed roots. The muskrat was not a carnivorous animal like a mink or wolf. If this hole was to freeze up the entire family would perish with no place to feed or rest.

Wanton destruction of the muskrat was caused by a number of things: unstable water levels either freezing or flooding them out and the illegal use of muskrat spears. The spear was used by out-of-season poachers who destroyed hundreds of houses by thrusting the spear through the top of the house, impaling the animal. The damage was done when the house was cut open to retrieve the muskrats. The hole through the ice, their life line, would then freeze up. The muskrat population was soon decimated.

# Fort St. Charles

In 1732 the French voyageur, LaVerendrye, reached Lake of the Woods while searching for the Northwest Passage. Using the map of an Indian guide named Auchagah, he built the first trading post on Lake of the Woods on the shores of what is now called the Northwest Angle. Auchagah had told him of water to the west that was ill-tasting (sea water) and moved back and forth (tide). LaVerendrye came to the conclusion that Auchagah was describing the ocean.

Hoping to continue his explorations further to the west he planned to fortify the new trading post, Fort St. Charles, with wooden palisades—enclosing a chapel and barracks for the fort's garrison.

Although the general location of the fort was known for years it was not until 1908 that the site was definitely established on the south shore of Northwest Angle Inlet.

Camping on American Point, I remember my friend George Arnold Jr. (his dad owned American Point) and I rowing a small boat down to where Fort St. Charles had been located. We landed on the timber shoreline and began searching in the trees and willows. I remember we finally found a crude cross marking a mound of moss and soil. It was the remains of the original site of Fort St. Charles.

It appears to me that the shoreline probably changed in the two hundred years since LaVerendrye established the fort. A replica of Fort St. Charles can be visited on the same site as the original fort. To Monsignor Langevin, Archbishop of St. Boniface in Canada, belongs the honor of bringing to a successful conclusion efforts to preserve this historic site.

The story of Fort St. Charles and a Lake of the Woods island called Massacre Island is a fascinating

## 4 TIME TO FISH—TIME TO DRY NETS

tale that has never received its true place in history. In order for us to understand how such a tragedy could happen we have to understand that Lake of the Woods was debatable grounds during those years. The Cree Indians inhabited the lakes and forest districts of the Lake. The Sioux and other Indians controlled Buffalo Point and the grounds north to Reed River. Considered Western Plains Indians, the Sioux and other tribes continually carried out fierce tribal warfare in this area. The French-Canadians in this district were often times compelled to make a stand against the onslaught of Indians of all parties to whom the white men were a common enemy.

In 1736 explorer LaVerendrye had been waiting at Fort St. Charles for the arrival of supplies with which he hoped to continue his explorations further west. Food was so scarce for the garrison of the fort that it was decided to send back a body of men to the eastern forts for supplies.

On June 5th, 1736, within Fort St. Charles, the party selected made preparations for departure. The head of the party was Lieutenant Jean LaVerendrye, twenty-three year old son of the explorer. In the company with him was Father Aulneau, thirty-one year old Jesuit missionary, and nineteen other men. It was early afternoon on the beach below the fort when the voyageurs finished loading the three large canoes, each capable of carrying seven men with all their baggage.

Traveling east the canoes soon passed out of sight as the singing voyageurs paddled down Northwest Angle Inlet and turned south after rounding American Point. They were now in wide open waters of the Little Traverse.

Massacre Island is only eighteen miles from the site of Fort St. Charles, an easy afternoon paddle.

After getting beyond Massacre Island there is wide open water for thirty miles until you get into the mouth of the Rainy River. I believe weather conditions either slowed them down, or the waves rolling in from Big Traverse threatened their frail craft. Experienced travelers, they did not want to be caught out in the middle of the Big Traverse in their Indian canoes.

Whatever the reason, they decided to take refuge on Massacre Island, an island measuring about three-quarters of a mile in length and about a quarter of a mile wide. We can also assume the landing had been peaceful enough, but who can tell what ominous portents caused them to stop there for the night. The Frenchmen made their camp, campfires were lit, their last frugal meal was eaten, sentinels were placed, and the tired voyageurs lay down to sleep.

Some historians believe that they expected the assault but I do not believe that. If they expected trouble from the Indians, they would have turned around and made a run for the safety of the fort. They were all experienced and familiar enough with Lake of the Woods to paddle back to the fort in the dark with little difficulty.

It appears to me that the attack was planned ahead. The Indians were in and out of Fort St. Charles enough to know the expedition was planned to cross Lake of the Woods on their way to Rainy River. It seems unlikely that such a large war party of Indians would be waiting to ambush the expedition without planning the attack ahead of time. As soon as the expedition left Fort St. Charles, its progress was probably under the scrutiny of Indian scouts. It would take a fleet of two-man canoes to carry a war party large enough to assault an armed party on that island. The Frenchmen were trained soldiers with modern weapons compared to the Indian's tomahawks, bows, and arrows. If Lieutenant LaVerendrye expected the attack, he could have held them off saving at least some of his men. It looks like a sneak attack, during the night, by a large war party. The terrible tragedy was carried out in a few minutes. Indians later returned and looted the remains of the camp.

Friendly Indians probably carried the story of the massacre to Fort St. Charles the next day, but it was not until September 17th, 1736, that LaVerendrye dared to weaken Fort St. Charles by sending his men to Massacre Island to recover the remains of his murdered son, Father Aulneau, and the other nineteen men that had left three months before. If LaVerendrye could have sent a rescue party to Massacre Island earlier, it is possible they would have found clues or even a survivor.

Very few distinguishing features could be found to determine one man from another. Kindly hands, however, had covered the bodies of Father Aulneau and the young LaVerendrye under tumulus boulders, minus their heads which were carried away by the Indians. The two bodies and nineteen heads were removed to Fort St. Charles and buried in the chapel of the fort on September 17th, 1736.

A shroud of mystery surrounded the case from the beginning. Usually history finds its answers from survivors or from stories handed down from one generation to another, which never happened in this case. There were no clues from the voyageurs. It seems strange that their baggage, personal items, guns, and clothing were never recovered and returned by friendly Indians to the fort.

# Fort St. Charles

What happened to the three 25-foot canoes that left Fort St. Charles with stern flags flying and chansons floating on the breeze?

As news always travels fast we can assume that every Indian from the Cree and Sioux tribes knew of the massacre in a matter of days. Because the white man was a common enemy, the Indians never did divulge the reasons nor the details of that terrible night.

It was not until 1890, or 154 years after the event, that any organized effort was made to locate Massacre Island. Many generations of Indians have passed away or been scattered by fierce tribal warfare since the passing of LaVerendrye.

# 2

## Early Days and Fire Days

The name "Rat Portage" (Kenora) existed long before the advent of any white man. Called the country of the *Waszush*(muskrat) in the language of the Indian, it designated all of the area of the north side of Lake of the Woods at the outlet of the lake into the Winnipeg River in Canada. That area of the lake was spoken of by the Indians as, "the road to the muskrat country at the north end of the lake."

The swamps and backwaters were full of water grasses and great areas of wild rice. The habitat was ideal for the prolific muskrat as well as for the harvest of wild rice by the various Indian tribes.

The surface area of Lake of the Woods is 950,400 acres, making it the 40th largest lake in the world even considering such giants as the Great Lakes and the Caspian Sea. Containing some 14,000 islands, it is approximately 60 miles wide and 70 miles long. The United States owns 32.3% (307,010 acres) of the lake and the balance is in Canada.

## Early Days and Fire Days

The treaty with Great Britain in 1783, along with the Treaty of Ghent in 1814, defined the national boundary between the United States and Canada. The Great Lakes adapted themselves readily, except that they did not extend themselves entirely across the continent to the Pacific Ocean. The participants had to find a line from the northwest corner of Lake Superior so they extended the boundary from Lake Superior to a point at the northwestern tip of Lake of the Woods and then go north to the 49th parallel and follow that line to the Pacific. In 1824 a more accurate survey created a startling surprise. It disclosed that the northwest point of Lake of the Woods is actually north of the 49th parallel. So the line went north to the northwest point of Lake of the Woods which left the Northwest Angle (130 square miles) wholly unattached and disconnected from the rest of the United States.

This large area is called Angle Township and is an unorganized township that has no trustees or other officers. It is under the jurisdiction of Lake of the Woods County with county offices in Baudette, Minnesota. The Angle, along with all of Lake of the Woods and adjoining land, once belonged to Red Lake Indian Reservation; but now Red Lake only has jurisdiction over the unhomesteaded interior land.

This conspicuous "jog" in the boundary line, from the 49th parallel north through Lake of the Woods, made American Point in the Northwest Angle the farthest point north in the United States. When Alaska became a state, American Point lost that distinction.

At the time the French gave it their name, the Lake was well known by all the Indians thereabouts as *Min-es-tic*, which in their language means Lake of the Islands.

The Indian word for wood is *mis-tic* and the great similarity of sound of the words was readily confounded by the French, whose knowledge of the Indian language could only be acquired conversationally, which caused the name of the lake to be changed by them from Lake of the Islands to Lake of the Woods.

After 1740, the Hudson's Bay Company and the Northwest Fur Company were fiercely competing for Lake of the Woods fur trade. Dealing with the Indians was difficult because of tribal warfare. The pages of history of this territory were stained with blood. For Indians, priests, railroad builders, and gold seekers Lake of the Woods has been the scene of disaster and triumph. Up to 1870 this lake district was only exploited for its fur possibilities. The fur was collected up at Rat Portage and then started the long journey to Hudson Bay on its way to England.

When my grandfather Chris Guhl and his family arrived at Warroad in 1896, Lake of the Woods area was a land of opportunity. Rich in game, furs, rivers, lumber, land, and minerals. To many new arrivals, like grandpa, it was a profitable experience.

In the early days of natural resources the exploitation of the original stand of timber was the first to be used during that period of rapid resource use. After that problems began to mount. The land was not highly productive agriculturally, and the climate was rigorous. One author, writing on the heels of the Great Depression in 1942, wrote the following bitter statement:

> "The Big Bog of northern Minnesota is a vast expanse of almost flat wilderness-burned-over, cut-over covering two million acres which reach north from Red Lake to Rainy River and Lake of

## Early Days and Fire Days    11

the Woods, stretching east and west across four huge counties. A harsh and desolate land, it carries a soggy green remembrance of the ancient Lake Agassiz whose waters drowned it for thousands of years after the last great ice-sheet retreated northward, and in whose bed the lush vegetative growth of centuries has now formed the largest peat fields in the United States. The area was the scene of an ill-conceived drainage boom during the First World War, and as a result it became, in the following decade, the graveyard of twenty thousand dead hopes, a rural slum of fire-scarred forest and low-growing marsh jungle from which hundreds of duped settlers had already moved but in which hundreds of others stayed on to fight the pitches battle- doomed to defeat but containing elements of grandeur- against the encroaching swamp, the skimpy soil, the raging blizzards of winter, the enormous distance which separated them from markets, the loneliness and silence.

"By the Thirties, the area and the people trapped in it had become a major public problem. The settler's income had declined until most families, and frequently they were large ones, received less than $300 a year; taxes went unpaid while, on the other hand, relief problems were intensified, the four big wilderness counties were being crushed into bankruptcy, under the burden of providing schools, roads, and other facilities for the settlers, and "burn-outs" became steadily more frequent as settler's clearing fires got out of control and swept in blazing anger across the dried out swamps. But still the settlers stayed, stubborn hundreds of them, finding it impossible to forsake the desolate earth hallowed by years of their agonized labor, since to do so would be to admit a final, abysmal defeat beyond which further struggle, even breathing, would seem futile. They were sustained by an acid pride which required that they have some better place to go, and some better thing to do-a new opportunity clearly defined which could be considered a consequence of their struggle-before they abandoned land which was now a part of their being, made so by years of sweat and tears..."

While there are some unfair statements about the settlers, other statements are more accurate than most of us would ever admit.

Economic and resource management problems never did go away. Differences of opinion over management of Lake of the Woods resulted in bitter political confrontation in Roseau and Lake of the Woods Counties since the big lake's first commercial fishing began in the late 1800's.

Railroad transportation was not available until the 20th century. The Canadian National Railroad was built across this area in 1901, the same year the town of Warroad was incorporated. Roseau County did not experience rapid growth; and it is interesting to see that in 1958, forest and woodlands covered 70% of the county area. Of this acreage 6 to 7% of the total land was federally owned and 60% of the federal land in the area was under Indian Trust. There is still a high percentage of State and Federal land.

In 1930 a land program called the Land Resettlement Project affected subsequent settlement patterns in southeastern Roseau and southwestern Lake of the Woods County. In 1934, 310 families (1,050

# Early Days and Fire Days

persons) lived on the portion of these counties now in Beltrami Island State Forest and the Red Lake Wildlife Management Area. In 1933, their average annual family cash income from all sources, including farming, sale of forest products, government employment, other wage labor, and relief was $317. Farms averaged twenty-seven acres of cultivated land, and soils in the area were of very low productivity. Much of the original timber had been cut and marketed. Schools, roads, medical services, and churches ranged from low quality to nonexistent.

It was felt that, meager even by the standards of the 1930's, the area did not supply the minimum physical needs of these people for food, clothing, and shelter. They lacked sufficient cash income to pay for their public service. The government bureaucrats decided the families in this area absorbed $20,000 to $30,000 per year above what they paid in taxes for the support of schools, roads and relief, partly because the settlers often were responsible for high forest fire losses.

In 1934, it is true that in that area now called the Beltrami Island State Forest, fire consumed thousands of acres of forest and peat bogs because of the dry conditions. Peat was the most difficult to extinguish because it smoldered underground and was hard to detect. In most cases peat fires simply burned until the patch of peat bog was burned out.

I question the bureaucrat's estimate that each settler, in that area, cost the government $20,000 to $30,000 per year above what they paid in taxes because I worked as a fire fighter for the Minnesota Forestry for three months during school vacation. There were no trained fire fighter crews like today. Instead the State could muster all able-bodied men for fire duty if they needed the help.

# 14   TIME TO FISH—TIME TO DRY NETS

It was a sort of shanghai operation that operated with a truck instead of loading them on a ship. The law allowed the forest rangers to compel men to fight fire. Before you knew what happened, you were carrying water cans, digging firebreaks, establishing fire lines to back-fire on, and patrolling fire breaks with a shovel over your shoulder. For this work the State of Minnesota paid you fifteen cents per hour and I do not think we had any insurance. At the amount of wages they paid I doubt it cost the government $20,000 to $30,000 per year for each settler's public service.

It was an interesting summer for me with one experience still vivid in my memory: Warroad's District Ranger, Dick Willems, was in charge of the Clear River Station, 10 miles south of Warroad in the Beltrami section. Pulling me off of firebreak patrol we drove back to Warroad in his Model A Ford where we loaded up a wooden case full of dynamite sticks along with the caps and a roll of dynamite fuse. Tossing all of it into the back seat of the Ford we roared back past Clear River and out into the middle of a forest fire burning out of control. The smoke was so thick we were bouncing along off of the road more than we were on it.

I could not help but look back to where our dynamite was bouncing up and down as we sailed over tree stumps and ditches. Holding on for dear life I thought if the case of dynamite goes off no one in the world would ever know what happened to Dick and me.

Somehow or other in all that smoke we found the small meadow he was looking for and we began digging a hole with our shovels. Dick, said, "I know there is water here and we will blow a big hole to

## Early Days and Fire Days

serve as a reservoir. I will then move pumping equipment in to try and control this fire."

Working hard we managed to dig a hole six or seven feet deep and were so exhausted we could not dig anymore. We could not breathe without covering our nose and mouth with our wet handkerchiefs. I unloaded the dynamite down into the hole while Dick taped the sticks into one bundle, attaching the caps and the fuse. We then shoveled the dirt back into the hole and found a huge windfall to hide behind for "the Big Bang".

After Dick lit the fuse we dove behind the windfall and waited for the expected shower of water but that did not happen. Instead a cloud of dirt and rocks fell around us. When the dust settled we ran over to the crater which was 20 to 30 feet across but only 10 feet deep. It was completely dry—no sign of water.

Back in Dick's Ford we retraced our steps back to the gravel road to Warroad. The only thing we gained was the dynamite was no longer bouncing around in the back seat.

For a young seventeen-year old it was a fun summer. The forestry people established a camp for us at the Clear River Station. Army tents and best of all a cook shack under the charge of two Warroad women. Everything they cooked was delicious and if we were assigned to firebreak patrol they would send out hot food for lunch.

President FDR's Civilian Conservation Corps also maintained a large camp in the Beltrami Forest Reserve. One section was Black, all young men, from down in the "deep South" under the command of regular Army officers. The Civil Conservation Corps was segregated, the same as the Army, so the Blacks had their own camp.

# 16     TIME TO FISH—TIME TO DRY NETS

Using bulldozers we had contained the partly burned-over swamp and peat land to three hundred acres. The fire turned critical again when the wind turned into gale forces from the south. At daylight we were rushed back to try and keep it from jumping the firebreak and spreading throughout the jack pine forest towards Bemis Hill. The firebreak was four to five feet deep and ten feet wide at the top. My boss was Fred Moyer, a neighbor of mine from Warroad. We were assigned a section of the firebreak on the downwind side, a hopeless assignment.

Because the south wind created a dangerous situation the C.C.C. camp sent over a detachment of men from the Black section to help us. They liked neither us, the forest fire, or anything else about Minnesota. When Fred asked them to help us patrol the fire break they said, "No way, man, are we going into that sea of smoke and ashes because you white boys set that fire so you could get a job putting it out!"

# 3

## Grandpa Guhl—Commercial Fishing

Grandpa Guhl arrived in Warroad in 1896 with his wife Sofia and his five children: baby Anna Belle, Frank, Helena, Mabel, and Stella. Leaving their farm in Fosston, they traveled with two covered wagons to Crookston on the first leg of their journey to War Road. Warroad actually had two names at that time, the white settler's name and the native American's name, "War Path". It was the first large town any of the children had ever seen.

My mother Mabel said, "Pa stopped in front of a store to buy supplies. Huddling in the wagon we could not believe our eyes, the store's door had a glass window in it! That such a fanciful door existed was unreal to us. During the day we all walked along behind the wagon except Mother and baby Anna Belle."

The trip was hard on Sofia and Anna Belle, each day seemed to drain away a little more of their strength. They both had consumption (TB) and neither one of them would survive that first dreadful winter.

# 18    TIME TO FISH—TIME TO DRY NETS

Very little was known about consumption except it was usually fatal. The doctor in Fosston said the clean, dry air around Lake of the Woods could benefit their health. It is believed they caught the disease from drinking cow's milk contaminated with tuberculin bacillus.

The most difficult leg of their journey was from Roseau to Warroad, fighting swamps, narrow trails, hordes of mosquitoes, bull flies, and rain showers. They struggled for seven days building a road wide enough to get their covered wagons through. Arriving at Moody's Point, where the present DeMolee home is, they were greeted by the entire white population of Warroad, three families. The arrival of the new family called for a celebration so it was decided to have a dance in Moody's living room. Watching the party from the top of the stairs, my mother and her sisters felt happy and welcome. The next morning the whole family followed the trail along the river, anxious to see Lake of the Woods.

Walking down Lake Street they saw the Jones & Lawson Trading Post and Indian canoes pulled up on the river bank. Indian tepees, covered with animal skins, could be seen pitched close to the water's edge. Along the river they saw an Indian burial ground covered with tiny birch bark shelters containing fish hooks, bowls of corn, and bow and arrows. Everything was intended to make the "Happy Hunting Ground" everlasting. In the true spirit of the day, the Cugnet family provided them with a snug log cabin to live in during that first winter.

For young children, like Mabel and Stella, the winter was long and boring after the death of Sofia and Anna Belle. Frank and Grandpa were gone for days at a time working in the woods with their team of horses.

## Grandpa Guhl—Commercial Fishing

Aunt Helena married timber man Jack Comlins. So Mother, twelve years old, was now housekeeper for Grandpa Guhl and Frank.

Mother's favorite story about that winter was about Stella's and her experience while waiting for their father one day. Hearing footsteps they rushed to open the door only to find an old Indian man standing there. His forehead was covered with scar tissue and he was bald headed. Taking one look at him the girls crawled under a bed so frightened they could not move. Holding out a fresh piece of moose meat, they knew he came as a friend. Their visitor, called Ayashwas, was the chief of the Warroad and Buffalo Point tribes. A kindly old man, he had stopped by their cabin to help them out. He was a great warrior in the fierce battle between his people and the Sioux. On a ridge called Two Rivers, over fifty years before, he was scalped and left for dead on the battlefield.

That first winter was difficult with the whole family crowded into a single room. The kindness of the local Indians saved them by bring them venison, rabbits, and moose meat. That winter a bond was formed between the local Indians and our family that lasted through three generations.

Like other pioneers, Grandpa's first years in Warroad were tragic. He lost his wife, baby daughter, and his only son, Frank, in his first seven years after moving to Warroad. Frank at 17 years old was a lake victim along with two friends of his, Benjamin and Conrad Arnesen.

In the last days of October, 1903, Frank left his camp at Willow Creek and paddled his birch bark canoe to Warroad where he met his two friends. Both young men, they were returning to Rocky Point after working in the Red River Valley on thrashing crews.

## TIME TO FISH—TIME TO DRY NETS

Loading their gear into his canoe, they left for Rocky Point the next morning. It was a 12-mile paddle along the South Shore, not a long or difficult trip with a canoe. It was cold enough to freeze shell ice along the shore. Grandpa and my Mother were staying at Rocky Point where Grandpa was helping Barney Arnesen pull out his pond nets. The following day they found Conrad's jacket tangled up in a net. They immediately set sail for Warroad in Grandpa's sailboat, the *Grizzly*.

Searching along the South Shore they found Frank's canoe washed up on the beach, not far from Rocky Point. One cross bar was broken and it appeared that when one of them was shifting position they leaned on the cross bar, when it broke the canoe capsized.

The first body found was Frank's, in three feet of water where he was doubled up with cramps from exposure to the cold water. His shirt was covered with pitch from the canoe. It appeared he made it to the sand bar but his legs cramped up before he reached dry land. His two friends were found nearby. Exposure and cold water was also the cause of their death.

After Frank's death, Grandpa made his first trip to Canada where he was employed up north in the Canadian Arctic. My brother Dorrance remembers an early photograph from that trip showing Grandpa bundled up in furs driving a dog team. Unfortunately that photo was lost. On his second trip to Canada in 1905, he was joined by Frank Clement, a local teamster. They were hired for the summer to work on the Canadian Railroad system somewhere near Kenora, on the north end of Lake of the Woods. After the first spring thaw they loaded up their bobsleds for the long trip across Lake of the Woods. One sled

## Grandpa Guhl—Commercial Fishing

was used to haul oats and hay for the horses while the other sled carried a small caboose to camp in. As the crow flies it was an 80-mile trip.

Working all summer on railroad grades, they continued to work until freeze-up. Short of hay they used their canoe to look for a meadow to cut and stack hay for winter. Finding a small tributary stream they followed it until their canoe grounded on what they thought was a sand bar or a submerged log. Cutting into the obstacle with his axe he discovered it was a soft metallic metal. Chopping out a few chunks, it was soft and malleable enough to shape into lead line sinkers for gillnets. Shaking hands they agreed that neither one would return without the other, nor divulge their find. They planned to return to Canada the next year and stake out their claim.

After freeze-up they drove their horses back to Warroad across the ice. That summer Frank Clement was working for the railroad when he had a terrible accident. He slipped under a railroad car and both of his legs were cut off. With Frank maimed, they were unable to return to Canada the next year and as time went by they lost interest in returning to Canada as prospectors. It is possible they could have found a tin or lead deposit. Someplace near Kenora that lobe of metal is still there, intact except for a few notches Frank and Grandpa cut out with their axe 90 years ago.

In 1879 the Canadian Pacific Railway had changed Kenora from a single-dwelling trading post to a busy town of sawmills, warehouses, stores and fisheries. The only port on Lake of the Woods to have rail service at that time, it saw the beginning of the commercial fishing industry. With this fresh-fish outlet, commercial fishing began to thrive on the American side of the lake. Businessmen began to realize something of the enormous food supply the virgin lake could produce. The commercial fishery did not develop in ernest in Warroad until 1901 when the Canadian National Railroad built a line on the south side of Lake of the Woods. American fish companies like Booth, Baltimore, Finke, Ried, and Sandusky employed hundreds of men in the Warroad and Rainy River area.

Using crushed ice on the top and bottom of the fish, each wooden fish box weighted more than 100 pounds. Sturgeon, walleye pike, goldeyes and white fish were loaded on barges to be towed to Kenora or Warroad by company tugs. Bonded American fish could not be sold in Canada. Each box was re-iced and shipped by express to Chicago and New York. My Grandpa and the other commercial fishermen caught tons of sturgeon making Lake of the Woods famous for the sturgeon roe, called caviar. This expensive food was made famous by gourmets in Chicago and New York and Lake of the Woods was the major supplier in America. It was an important part of the fisherman's income at that time.

According to Minnesota statues at that time, fifty pound nets, and eighty fyke nets could be licensed on Lake of the Woods after 1900. In 1912 the statue was changed to allow 80,000 feet of gillnet gear. Each license holder was allowed 4000 feet of gillnets. The new statute required that each fisherman be licensed to operate certain type of gear in a designated location. The original company fisheries and their pound nets disappeared, with the small, independent gillnet operators the only ones left on the lake.

Open and closed seasons for commercial fishing as well as sport fishing were now enforced. New taxes, permits and reduced licenses plagued every fisherman, making it more difficult to make a living. Lake of the Woods continued its tremendous commercial harvest of fish until the fishery was closed in 1985. In 1955-1968, the Minnesota DNR poundage records show Lake of the Woods commercial harvest at 34.3 million pounds and Ontario at 28.7 million pounds, with tullibee and suckers being the highest poundage. The fish species in this report, lumped together, are: bullheads, burbot, perch, saugers, suckers, tullibee, whitefish, northern pike and walleye pike for a Minnesota and Ontario grand total of 63 million pounds of fish caught in that period. In that same period the annual game harvest in American waters was 214,000 pounds of walleye pike and 140,000 pounds of the other game fish.

Because Lake of the Woods is shallow, gillnets were always lifted by hand. This traditional way to lift nets never changed in a century of netting fish. Maximum depth in the Big Traverse, on the American side, is only 35 to 40 feet. Protective of their freedom, the commercial fishermen were tough, resourceful, and so independent they were never able to organize, even for their own survival. Even the commercial fishing critics acknowledged their independent and gritty spirit back in the days when it was more highly valued than it is today. Most of the Warroad "lake men" came from commercial fishing clans with names like Arnesen*, Brewster*, Vickaryous*, Moyer*, Parker*, Hilborne*, Saurdiff*, Ringling*, Carlquist*, Selvog*, Boucha, Wenzel, Springsteel, Giddens, Pick, Meyers, Arnold, Hoover, and my family, the Guhl's* and Johnston's.

**24     TIME TO FISH—TIME TO DRY NETS**

The above commercial fishermen marked with an asterisk lost their own lives or a member of their family by drowning on Lake of the Woods. Commercial fishing is a dangerous occupation, still at the top of the insurance companies charts.

In my family, our two boys Alan and Arthur grew up believing that "fishing was in their blood." They were out helping me lift gillnets while still in grade school. They, the fourth generation of my family, would be the last to commercially fish the American side of the lake when new statutes and regulations destroyed the industry in 1985. The Canadian side still operates a Lake of the Woods commercial fishery in Ontario. The price of walleye pike to the consumer increased and availability decreased when the Department of Natural Resources banned the commercial harvest of game fish on the American side of the lake.

Busy dock scene at Booth Fishery's pier located on Warroad River, near the railroad bridge. Note there is no water tower, nor uptown grain elevator. Photo: Warroad Heritage Center.

***Top:*** Dock scene at Oak Island early 1900's. The *Na-Ma-Puk* is the outside boat across the end of the dock. The tug with its bow on shore is ready to load pound nets. There is a ramp with a loading incline on the bottom center of picture that was used to drag the heavy tarred nets on board. Next is a tiny tripod called a twine reel. A ream of mending twine is on the reel.
***Bottom:*** U.S. Dredge being pulled with oxen. Where this picture was taken is unknown. However, it states the dredge was on Lake of the Woods, Warroad, Minnesota. Photos, Warroad Heritage Center.

*Top:* Commercial fisherman, Hans Selvog, with another Lake of the Woods sturgeon at Booth Fishery located uptown on the Warroad River. Weight, 120 pounds dressed. Hans is holding its tail. Probably taken around 1913. Note the loose fish in the bottom of the pound boat indicating he did not travel very far after catching the sturgeon. *Bottom:* Loading fish at the CN railroad depot, in Warroad. Note the old water tower top left. Model T Ford trucks indicate about 1914. Photos, Warroad Heritage Center.

*Top:* One day's catch of twelve Lake of the Woods sturgeon at Booth Fishery, in Warroad. Booth Fishery manager Bert Steele is even holding one! Probably around 1912 or 1913.

*Bottom:* Bert Steele sitting by probably the largest sturgeon ever caught in Lake of the Woods. Hans Selvog caught it in 1913 at Elm Point, six miles north of Warroad. It was a 265 pounder. Photos, Warroad Heritage Center.

Photo from a postcard by Collins Studio in Warroad. This picture was taken uptown at Booth Fisheries. Steam tug ahead is the *Knute Nelson*. Standing in the pond net boat is commercial fisherman Hans Selvog. In the doorway of the fishery is Andrew Swenson. This sturgeon was 7 feet 2 inches in length, 176 pounds dressed weight. Round weight would be over 230. This fish probably came from the Elm Point area six miles north of Warroad harbor. Sturgeon was caught for its caviar and Lake of the Woods was the main source in America. Caviar, at 85¢ per pound, was the fisherman principal source of income at the time. The sturgeon meat was not valuable.

*Top:* Near Selvog Fishery, Warroad, Minnesota, 1949. This huge bear was shot by Chet Brown and Norm Hohn at the Northwest Angle. The bear skin is over seven feet long and it is estimated that it probably could have been a record for black bears in Minnesota. Left to right: Chet Brown, Jack Starren, Norm Hohn, tall man unknown, and Bud Stebor. Bush pilot Chet Brown along with Dayton Anderson died when their seaplane crashed during the night while they were flying to Hay Island.

*Bottom:* The first U.S. Engineer's Warroad Dredge, *U.S. Dredge Warroad*. Note the stern paddle wheel. Early 1900's picture taken in the mouth of the Warroad Harbor. Dredges like this were steam powered and able to move tons of dirt every day. Photos, Warroad Heritage Center.

*Top:* The old Selvog Fishery. In pioneer days it was called the Northwestern. Today it is a Casino. The Great Northern Railway built a rail siding from their main line to handle the fish tonnage. That siding is now a road named Taylor's Drive named after Warroad's former mayor, Morris Taylor. Photo, Margaret Marvin.

*Bottom:* The old Arnesen Fishery at Rocky Point, located on the South shore of lake of the Woods, it has been the home of the Arnesen family since 1897. It is now Arneson's Rock Harbor Resort.

My Grandfather, Chris Guhl, fisherman and philosopher, with my mother, Mabel, in 1933. Grandpa Guhl arrived at Warroad in 1897 with his wife and five children. Traveling in two covered wagons, he spent four days clearing the road from Roseau to Warroad trying to get his wagons through. They were the fourth white family to settle in what was then called War Road. He established a commercial fishing station at Willow Creek in 1902 operating fyke nets in that area. In 1903, disaster struck the family when his only son Frank and two Arnesen boys drowned when their Indian birch bark canoe tipped over while they were paddling to Rocky Point on October 27th. He fished at Willow Creek until 1916 when he filed on a homestead near Reed River in Buffalo Bay on Lake of the Woods. Building a cabin and smokehouse on what is now called Guhl's Point, he smoked goldeyes selling them for 12¢ per pound with a Norwegian friend, Andrew Moen. Grandpa died in Seattle, Washington in 1934 while visiting his daughter Stella.

*Top:* In 1900 the Warroad *Plaindealer* carried a story about the Guhl family and their three pets: a moose and two wolves. Living over on Guhl's Point, south of the Warroad River, Grandpa's son Frank found the puppies while running his trap line. The first time my dad saw my mother, one of the timber wolves was following her across the river while she was crossing on the ice.

*Bottom:* Grandpa Guhl's fish station on Guhl's point in Buffalo Bay. He and his brother Ferdinand smoked goldeyes until World War I, when as a German, he was not welcome in Canada. My mother Mabel, left, btother Dorrance, center, Aunt Stella, right.

*Top:* Grandpa Guhl's team of oxen with brother Dorrance and I sitting on the load of wood. Dad is driving. Oxen were used for heavy work. They were slow but could out-pull a team of horses. Grandpa worked with his team in the winter months. We were at Grandpa's on the south side of the Warroad River.

*Bottom:* Grandpa and I, in 1920, mending his fyke nets. He was already teaching me how to mend nets. He fished his fyke nets out of his camp at Willow Creek. Arriving in Warroad with his five children and wife in the late 1800's, they were one of the first white families to settle in Warroad before it was organized into a town. Grandpa Guhl died in Seattle, Washington, while visiting his daughter Stella. Morris Grove wrote in the Warroad Pioneer, "Chris Guhl was one of the most hospitable and lovable men I have ever known."

# 4

## Dad and Early Warroad Days.

      Dad's first name was Albert, middle name was Ernest, and family name was Johnstone. That is the way Grandma Johnston always spelled it. Not only did Dad drop the "e" but also the "t" when he became a businessman in Warroad and Roseau County. Roseau county was primarily settled by Swedes and Norwegians so Dad found it easier to do business with a good Swede name of Al Johnson. But for legal papers he continued to use Johnston. Growing up in Warroad people assumed that we were Swedes instead of English and German.

    Dad's first glimpse of Warroad was from the open door of a railroad cattle car while delivering a load of cattle to Winnipeg, Manitoba. With that job finished he "jumped a freight train" back to the U.S. where it stopped in Warroad to clear U.S. Customs and to take on water needed for the steam engine used to pull the train.

    With time on his hands he walked across the street to the saloon in the Lakewood Hotel. In 1902 it was Warroad's finest. He liked the looks of the

## Dad and Early Warroad Days.

town and was anxious to see beautiful Lake of the Woods before moving on. He decided to stick around and found a job making handmade cigars in Warroad's cigar factory. Only a few months after he began working in the cigar factory, he bought out the business. The first thing he changed was the brand name of his cigar from "Old Comrade" to "Lake of the Woods Cigars" with a picture of the steamboat *Keenora* on the box.

Cigarettes were not part of the tobacco business yet except a "roll your own" brand called Duke's Mixture. The tobacco was sold in a tiny cloth sack with a draw string to close it with. The sack sold for 5¢, including a pack of cigarette papers. The art of rolling your own took a lot of practice, but it was cheap so it became a best-seller generating millions of dollars for the Duke Family. Doris Duke, last of the family, became a spoiled rich girl that squandered the Duke fortune and came to a tragic end.

Duke's Mixture was promoted as the smoke of outdoor "he-men" by showing the yellow Duke's Mixture tag hanging outside the shirt pocket of a cowboy or other outdoor type. In the western movies it would show the cowboy riding his horse while rolling a cigarette with one hand. None of my friends could do that!

Duke's Mixture lost its share of the market when cigarettes like Wings became popular at 10¢ per pack. Other tobacco products like Snuff, Right Cut, and Spark Plug were trademark products of tobacco factories. Dill's Best, Sir Walter Raleigh, and King Edward were all popular pipe-smoking blends. Ladies did not use tobacco products like men did. Most men either smoked or chewed tobacco or used both.

When Prohibition became law in 1920, it was the end of the local cigar factories like Dad's. The local saloon was the main outlet for cigar sales so when Prohibition closed them, it was the end of not only his cigar business but of all small town cigar factories.

Before moving to Warroad in 1902, Dad had spent long intervals away from home and he was living the life of a nomad at 32 years old. Like all cowboys he enjoyed the solitude of life on the trail. An overnight stay in a cattle town, when they were near one, served to break the boredom of camp life.

A good looking man with a stiff brush of hair and bushy eyebrows he stood straight and tall even though he was only five-foot-five and one hundred thirty-five pounds.

Energetic and resourceful he was no longer satisfied with the freedom of life on the range. It was no longer as much fun as it used to be, he was looking for a place to settle down, have a family and live like other people. He always loved the outdoors and Warroad offered him the chance to live off the bountiful resources of Lake of the Woods.

Living with tough and sometimes unfriendly men, barroom brawls and bare-knuckle boxing was a way of life. They had taken a toll. His handsome face was flawed by cauliflower ears and a broken nose. He had a high level of pain tolerance, so in a bruising fight he just never gave up.

His beautiful blue eyes were large and changed color along with his mood. If he was angry they seemed to double in size changing color to a pale blue. His motto, "Hit 'em first, never argue," earned him a reputation in Roseau and Lake of the Woods Counties of never losing a fight. Newcomers to the

## Dad and Early Warroad Days.

area soon found out what the old timers already knew, "Don't fool around with Al."

It was not always that way. As a young man he learned to survive by boxing and wrestling around the camp fires while working on huge thrashing crews throughout the farm belt. His small size encouraged other men to challenge him, only to find his speed and skill would defeat them.

His first saloon party was a disaster he never forgot. Years later he told me about it:

> "My first trail job was with half a dozen cowboys driving a herd of cattle to a railroad terminal. After loading the cattle in boxcars, our job was done. It was the first money I had ever earned and I could not believe it when we were paid with gold. My pay was one gold coin and it was burning a hole in my pocket.
>
> "With the job done the crew decided to clean up and visit the town's only saloon. Clutching my gold coin in my fist I was filled with anticipation of the unknown, because I had never been inside a saloon before.
>
> "When the boys left for town they would not let me ride with them. 'Too young,' they said. So I was left alone at our camp. Near midnight I could no longer stand it so I decided to visit the saloon on my own. Peeking through the swinging doors, I could see it was full of people, some were gambling, others drinking and dancing with the saloon girls. My friends were drinking and playing pool across the room from the bar.
>
> "Excited about buying my first drink in a saloon, I placed my gold coin on top of the bar trying to impress the bartender that I was no

## 38  TIME TO FISH—TIME TO DRY NETS

freeloader. Busy with other customers he paid no attention to me.

"Before the bartender noticed me a sweet voice next to me asked, 'Is that your gold piece?' 'Yes it is,' I replied.

"She gestured towards the bartender, 'He will not serve young boys, and you look young to me. Why not pick up your gold coin and follow me upstairs to my room where we can party together. Nobody will find you there.'

"I thought, 'The drink can wait, but this woman is not going to.' Picking up my gold coin, and tucking it away in my pocket, I turned to her and said, 'Let's go.'

"She led the way to the stairway leading up to her room. We were half way up the stairs when I heard one of my gang shouting, 'Hey, there's Al going up the stairs with that girl. Come on let's teach him a lesson.'

"The whole gang came across the room and before I knew it they were carrying me over to a pool table. Climbing up on top of it two of the fellows caught a hold of my feet and began shaking me while I was hanging upside down. The only thing of value that I was carrying was my gold coin and they wanted it. When it fell out of my pocket it rolled right into the out stretched hands of my cowboy friends. 'Drinks for the house,' was the last thing I heard before they let me go."

After that experience, Dad, a prudent man, learned that he would be well-advised to never allow anybody to lay a hand on him. Nobody ever caught him off-guard again.

## Dad and Early Warroad Days.

His age did not diminish his skill in boxing and wrestling so there were always a few bullies that wanted to see if he was as good as his reputation. They usually ended up with their teeth knocked down their throat.

He never did live down the story about a traveling carnival playing in Baudette's town hall. It was the year before he was married, 1905, when he and a couple of his Warroad buddies rode the C.N. train to Baudette to take in the show. The carnival had the usual wrestling match, where their man would take on any and all comers from the audience for a cash prize. So far nobody could last long enough to win the $50 prize.

Watching one local after another take a licking, his friends urged him to take on the "pro".

They said, "You can take that bully, Al. Teach him a lesson."

Pulling off his jacket, Dad waited until the wrestler began stomping around the ring, flexing his muscles. When he passed him, Dad climbed through the ropes, picked him up and threw him through the window into the alley outside. Because of his size and speed he needed surprise to win.

It was not noticeable to most people but Dad walked with a slight limp because one leg was shorter than the other. Halfway between his knee and ankle he had a scar just off the center of his leg. When he was 15 years old he was working in a sawmill when a blade from a planer broke loose and sliced right through his leg. Pulling a door off of a building the men used it as a stretcher to carry Dad home. The doctor used silver pins to close the wound both on the front and back.

The wound festered and had to be lanced by the doctor every day or two. This was done by removing the silver pins to let the wound drain, then closing it up again with the pins. The doctor used only a strong antiseptic but no anesthesia was used on this procedure.

Before the doctor began he would clear everything away from Dad's bedside because the pain was so severe Dad threatened to kill him if he could get a hold of anything to do it with. After a few weeks he was up and around, with no after effects except that the leg did not grow anymore. He was always thankful that the doctor managed to save his leg for him.

When Dad moved to Warroad he heard that the Guhl family, that lived across the river, had a tame moose and two timber wolves that followed them around like a family dog. He did not think much about it until 1905 when he noticed a slender girl, Mabel Guhl, walking across the ice, followed by two timber wolves. While out hunting, Mabel's brother Frank had found two tiny, starving wolf puppies and brought them home for his sisters. Feeding them milk and scrap pieces of venison, Mabel and her sister Stella raised them. In 1900 the Warroad Plain Dealer carried the following news item: "The Guhl family has a tame moose and two timber wolves that follow them around wherever they go." Dad always said, "It is the only case on record that timber wolves acted as Cupid."

In 1906 Dad and Mother were married in Rainy River with his sister and her husband, attorney Jim Taylor, standing up for them.

Dad's sister Floss was one of the early school teachers in this area. Shorty after she married Jim Taylor, Warroad's first attorney at law, they moved to Hamilton, Montana, where Jim's law practice was more lucrative than in Warroad. Receiving a

## Dad and Early Warroad Days. 41

telegram that they were taking the train to Warroad for a visit, Mother began to plan a dinner party for this big event. Dorrance, Vernabelle, and I were excited. Jim being a lawyer was very impressive to us kids. We all worked helping Mom clean up the house getting ready for their visit. Mother planned a special meal for their first dinner and informed Dad that he would say grace. Not a church going man, Dad objected to doing it. But Mom said, "You ARE going to say grace for this special meal!"

When the big day arrived I wondered how Dad would make out in his new role. Us kids were bursting with curiosity wondering how Dad would handle it. Bowing my head I peeked up and knew something was about to happen because Dad's big blue eyes were reflecting more mirth then reverence. Bowing his head he said, "Three potatoes for four of us, thank God there's no more of us!"

Always popular with the young crowd that hung out at Joe Holland's pool hall, Dad enjoyed playing snooker with them. Snooker was his favorite game that required a higher degree of skill than straight pool. Always a soft touch, he would lend the crowd money if they needed it.

John Lightning, an Indian friend of mine, told me about an incident that happened to him when he was sixteen years old attending high school in Warroad:

> "Your Dad and I were playing snooker in Joe Holland's pool hall when a tall, rangy stranger walked in. It was obvious that he was a C.N. train passenger with a little time to spare while the engine took on water, express mail, and passengers at the depot just across the street.

# TIME TO FISH—TIME TO DRY NETS

"The stranger said, 'I will bet twenty dollars that I can beat anybody in a foot race around the block.'

"Your Dad laid down his pool cue and said, 'John, you can beat him, I'll back you.'

"I followed your Dad to the bar where he placed his twenty dollars along side the stranger's.

"'I've got a boy that can beat you,' your Dad said.

"I pulled myself up straight and looked the stranger straight in the eye. I was thinking, 'I don't know if I can beat him, but I am one scrawny Indian boy that is going to run like hell trying!' Everybody in the place was watching us standing there staring at each other. After a minute or two the stranger picked up his twenty dollar bill and walked out the door."

Dad, in 1950, with his grandchildren, Alan Johnston and Margaret Johnston (Mrs. Frank Marvin). They are a little gun shy of his pipe.

*Top:* Dad and his retriever, Teddy, in front of our house down Lake Street. In the fall I would wake up early in the morning when Dad would shoot a mess of ducks in Hospital Bay for supper. Teddy would retrieve them. The birch tree to the right grew up to be a giant. Dad's cigar factory is behind the house to the left.

*Bottom:* The other two fishermen in my family, our boys Alan and Arthur, on a camping trip at Hand Organ Point, near Knights Island. They were the fourth generation of my family to commercially fish Lake of the Woods.

# 5

# Diphtheria—Small Pox

In the dark ages of medicine, diphtheria was called "The Black Death." An acute infectious disease caused by bacterium and characterized by weakness and high fever, it caused the formation in the air passage of a membrane-like obstruction to breathing that in fatal cases caused the patient's complexion to turn dark blue. The toxic bacillus strain was the most serious, affecting young people usually in the fall and early winter season.

Although this story is about my family and diphtheria in 1922 when I was five years old, medicine was just beginning a program that would eradicate, in one generation, most of the contagious diseases with the use of free inoculations in the school and home. Only a few years before in 1884, a small pox epidemic struck the Indians on Rainy River. With no medical help, all the Indians on one reserve died with the exception of one woman and a baby. The baby's name was Ch-pe-zan (be quiet) and she died of measles in 1934.

# Diphtheria—Small Pox

In rural communities like Warroad, the health officials placed the home in quarantine, the most effective way to isolate them from the rest of the community. If your family had one of the yellow quarantine signs on your front door, you could not leave the premises nor could anyone visit you except the doctor. While under quarantine, all vocal contact was made through closed doors. With no person-to-person contact allowed, all mail, medicine, food and clothing needs were communicated by written notes that were posted on the outside of the door.

In the cities, families with diphtheria had an option, either the isolation ward in the hospital or be quarantined at home. If the latter option was used, the entire family's movements were restricted with the same consequences as small towns, nobody could go to work to support the family. As most people could ill-afford not to work, the home quarantine system was not used as much in the cities.

We were experiencing cold January weather in the month of December when Dorrance, my fifteen year old brother, complained to Mom about a sore throat. She knew it was serious when she noticed the enlarged glands on his neck. Dad hurried away to the hospital to bring Doctor Elliot home so he could take a look at it. Doctor Elliot, a World War I veteran, was a well trained physician that just happened to be in Warroad at the right time. All rural doctors, like Elliot, not only made house calls, but they treated most of their patients in their own beds at home.

With only a couple of blocks to go it did not take Dad long to return with Doctor Elliot in tow. They walked like everybody else in town, following the narrow paths or tracks made by bobsleds hauling firewood used to heat the school and all other buildings in town. Rural residents who needed help used a pony pulling a "cutter" or toboggan to pick up the doctor when he made house calls out in the country.

While Mom showed the doctor Dorrance's upstairs room, sister Vernabelle, age ten, and I waited downstairs in our favorite place around the heating stove in the middle of our living room.

When they came back downstairs, Dr. Elliot said, "Diphtheria. I will be back and place a quarantine sign on your house. None of you are to leave this house. You may go out into your yard, provided there are no other persons around you." With no water or indoor plumbing in the houses, that freedom of movement was appreciated by the quarantined families.

Checking Vernabelle's tonsils, he found a dull inflammatory zone in her throat, while the same examination showed no signs of infection in my throat. He said, "Vernabelle is coming down with it, but Alvin should be moved out of the house at once."

Dad and Mom decided to take me across the river to Aunt Helena's home, located on Guhl's Point which was across the river from Selvog's fishery (this is not the same Guhl's Point as in Buffalo Bay.) She lived there all alone in a two story house that she and her husband, Jack Collins, had built when they were married.

Jack made his living as an entrepreneur timber man dealing with the railroads. A flamboyant character, some years he would make a fortune selling timber to the railroads; next year he might lose it. A jaunty, smiling young man, he mesmerized his associates flashing a huge diamond stick pin, top hat and a gold-topped cane.

Years later my friend, Sever Selvog, told about the time Jack was in Winnipeg and needed money to

## Diphtheria—Small Pox    47

buy timber. He paid for it with a sight draft on Sever's Warroad bank account. After waiting for a month for Jack to pay it back, Sever said, "Thinking the money was lost he felt he would never see Jack again." He was just getting ready to take the train to Winnipeg and find him when Jack walked into his office carrying a satchel full of money. A pleasant and smiling Jack paid him back the loan.

Charged with manslaughter in 1908, he was found not guilty in the death of an employee, Andrew Coleman, who had fallen off a bobsled used to haul lumberjacks to the Comlin's Timber Company's camp near Graceton. A few years later, he moved to the Twin Cities leaving everything behind except his red-headed secretary.

He became a bondsman specializing in making bonds for criminal offenders, who would pay him an exorbitant fee to make bail for them so they could get out of jail. When my brother Dorrance, was attending University of Minnesota, he used to visit him. Jack was doing fine in the bondsman business. He was driving a Duesenberg convertible and still had his red-headed secretary.

By the time Mom had me all bundled up for the trip to Helena's, I was in a tantrum caused by frustration at leaving my family. Kicking and crying, Dad carried me out and tucked me into a box that he had secured to the sled platform. At the river bank, he gave me a shove and I sailed down the bank (no cement wall then) and on to the river in Hospital Bay. We followed the old river channel to Helena's, where she showed me to my upstairs room. it would be the first time I ever slept alone in my own room.

Alone and afraid at night, the thick goose down feather tick kept me snug and warm. Pulling it over head made me feel safe and secure in that strange room. The only chore she gave me was to feed her flock of white geese. I was terrified of them because the big ganders would hiss and chase me every time I came into the chicken coop.

After a couple of days, Helena told me, "Dorrance is critical and Doctor Elliot is going to try the new diphtheria anti-toxin that he had just received." The dosage was large, over 100,000 units of antitoxin injected into Dorrance's back. The large syringe used was a novelty to most people, in fact, Dorrance kept his as a souvenir. By the next day, Dorrance's fever was down and in a few days he was out of danger. Vernabelle did not mend as fast because her high fever made her so weak. It was spring before she was able to get back on her feet.

Every two or three days, Helena took me over to the doctor's office for checkups. One day he said, "Take off your shirt." Before I had a chance to cry, I received my shot in the back. A week later, he allowed me to move back home on Christmas Day. By New Year's Day, the quarantine was lifted from our home, allowing Dad to go back to work buying fur throughout Roseau County.

The next year, an improved toxin was given to all school children. The improved type was an arm shot, probably similar to what is used today. The only good thing about that first shot was that I did not have to take another when my first grade class received them.

The old Carlquist home down Lake Street was Warroad's first hospital. It was renovated with the doctor's office and operating room located on the ground floor. Small and understaffed, it did not have an isolation ward for contagious diseases like diphtheria. In our hospital, the doctor carried the patient to the ward upstairs after surgery or delivering a

## Diphtheria—Small Pox

baby. When my wife, Alberta, and my sister-in-law, Eudora, worked there as Registered Nurses for Dr. Leitch in 1939, they worked the night shift alone taking care of patients and keeping the stove full of firewood.

# 6

## Basketball Was King—Playing Hockey.

The Great Depression in the 1930's affected everyone in the United States; however, cold winters, hot summers, economic hardship, along with little government assistance, spawned its beginning in Warroad in the 1920's. With little employment and no money, Warroad residents struggled to exist. An example of the times was Warroad's first public skating rink. With more man-power than money, the city fathers decided to enclose Warroad's first ice skating rink with cakes of ice instead of buying boards.

It was located across Lake Street from the present American Legion hall. Using horses and bob sleds, tons of river ice were piled two cakes high all around the new ring. It worked fine as far as flooding the rink went, but the ice cakes were hard if one "hit the boards". Every once in a while playing hockey, the puck would sail through a crack in the ice. Another problem developed during the spring thaw, the ice was slow to melt, creating a flood. I remember the road and sidewalk were flooded so we had to

## Basketball Was King—Playing Hockey. 51

go a block north to get to school. The next rink used more conventional methods using boards instead of ice cakes.

A warming house was provided and the care taker was Phil Huerd. The local hockey expert was Ralph Bennett. The rink charge was $1.50 for a season ticket or one dime per day. If you played on Ralph's hockey team, there was no charge. Without a dime or money for a season ticket I decided to try and make Ralph's hockey team. Free skating was the way to go.

Hanging around the warming house I had my chance one Saturday afternoon when Ralph could not find anybody to play goal. I volunteered and the leg pads and chest protector were strapped on me. I do not remember who we were playing but we won the game and Ralph Bennett felt I was the turning point with a few good saves.

He told Phil, "We have a goalie here. Did you see how he holds his legs, his strong hands?" Ralph was ecstatic and I was puzzled because I had no idea what I was doing.

Next weekend I was placed in the goal again against a tough, smart team. They slammed pucks at me from every direction with most of them going in the net. I could not believe what was happening, how was that puck getting in the net? On the way home I realized why; I was a poor goalie! My hockey career was brief but not all was lost: I skated free for two days!

Basketball was king in the Warroad School—there was no high school hockey at that time. When I was a sophomore in 1933, nobody had any money so money was not a problem. When you do not have something, you do not know what you are missing. School was important to our parents, they hoped education would open the door to the good life for their children. It was a different story to their children. School was something you had to attend or the truant officer would catch you. Of course, the truant officer has now disappeared, he now has the fancy name of Attendance Officer.

The idea of education in our school was different than it is today. High school was not compulsory so there was no pampering to keep you in attendance. With no school lunch program you walked home for noon lunch and hurried back to avoid a tardy mark on your report card. Until consolidation of the "one room, one teacher" country schools there was no school bus. If you lived in the rural area and attended high school you walked to school and back home again unless you were lucky enough to catch a ride. To the country students, extra-curricular activities were a sacrifice with many walking home in the dark, late at night.

However, basketball was the number one school sport. With a jump ball at center court after each basket, game points were low compared to today's game. When Gus Young, an excellent basketball player and coach was hired, basketball as we knew it was changed. Gus was a graduate from Carleton College, energetic, handsome, a classy dresser, and a demanding coach that expected excellence in the class room as well as on the basketball court.

Coach Young was a natural born showman and promoter. He outfitted the Warriors with snappy new uniforms and they were the only team in the region to sport matching warm-up suits. His razzle dazzle warm-ups looked like the Harlem Globe Trotters.

When his team hit the floor, they were going wide open, full speed ahead, no reverse. The fired-up players intimidated their competition with a wild

## Basketball Was King—Playing Hockey. 53

flurry of warm-up drills and battle cries. The visiting team stood gaping with open mouths while the Warroad fans stood up and cheered for their gallant Warriors. It was a sharp shooting team that was a joy to watch.

Hans Selvog, a commercial fisherman, perfected a technique to extract oil from the liver of the burbot, a rough scavenger fish from Lake of the Woods. The oil was tested and found to be as good or better than cod liver oil, one of the only vitamin pills on the market at that time. To make sure his team stayed in good physical condition, Coach Young made sure each player received a tablespoon full each day. It tasted very much like caster oil, the only medicine along with cough syrup and baking soda your mother kept in the home. Caster oil had the most unpleasant, nasty and nauseating taste that a human being could stand. When the team filed out of the locker room they passed a table with a jug of burbot liver oil for their required shot of vitamins for the day. The fact that it was free to the team assured the success of this health program.

With good coaching and good players, Warroad did not lose a game. We walked over our old, ancient foe, Roseau, with ease. I do believe in one game they only scored six points against the new Warriors. No more free throws using two hands and shooting from the waist. The team was taught to shoot with their arms, ball held high.

As with every good team Warroad soon had a super star. Charley Dumais was the best shot of anybody that ever played Warroad basketball. Zip, zip from every direction the ball sailed through the hoop without touching the rim. By the time the season ended he was high point man in the Region with a seventy percent free throw record. It was said that at practice one day he made fifty free throws without a miss.

The team peaked out at tournament time walking through the Subdistrict and the District with ease. For the first time and on up to this date, it was the only time Warroad was to get that far in basketball. With poor roads, no school buses and very little money, only a handful of parents and very few students were able to go and watch the team play in Crookston. Day-to-day school continued the same as usual, except if a student had a ride they would be excused to attend the tournament.

My friend, George Arnold Jr., owned a little old four cylinder Chevy two-seater. He was the only one in high school to drive his own car, in fact, a number of the students' parents did not own a car. Four of us piled into the little Chevy to follow the team to Crookston. It was a great adventure because none of us had traveled that far from Warroad before nor had we ever stayed in such a large town.

With almost no money, we found a walk-up rooming house that charged 75¢ per night double occupancy. Two stayed out of sight in the car while we checked in. After dark they slipped into the room for the night. We pooled our money and only had enough to buy tickets for the game along with a sack full of day-old pastry from a bakery.

Our first game was in the afternoon and when the four of us filed into the huge auditorium we could not believe any building could be that big. We were matched with Bemidji, one of the most powerful clubs in the state. The handful of Warroad fans did not fill one row of seats while the Bemidji fans filled one section. Our cheers were swallowed up along with our cheerleaders when the Bemidji team stormed out on the floor. You can imagine how

## Basketball Was King—Playing Hockey.

frightened our team was facing off with this powerhouse. Warroad lost to Bemidji and then to Ada for third place. Because they had used ineligible players both Bemidji and Thief River Falls were disqualified. Ada won the slot in the state tournament with Warroad runner-up.

Years later I had the pleasure of introducing Gus Young as guest speaker at the high school alumni banquet. Dutch Marshalk, Bill Marvin, Bruce Finger, Clarence Selvog and Charley Dumais, all members of that team were able to attend. Missing was John Lightning, Ed Stebore, Lorne Olson, Hugh McDonald, and Laurence Arnesen. After the banquet we all got together at Bill Marvin's home and talked over old times.

In 1934 Gus left Warroad to coach at his alma mater, Carleton College, and later professional basketball. But he never did forget Warroad and his friends here. Warroad has had some great coaches and teachers—Gus Young belongs at the head of the list.

# 7

## Fish Peddlers and Lamplighters

By the time I was eleven years old I knew the only way to have things was to earn money and buy them. My friend Frenchy Revaird and I decided to go into business for ourselves. The only business we could get into was the fish business—we would become fish peddlers. Making a deal with brother Dorrance and Dad for fish was the first step in our plan. We would turn the net reel every day and take fish for our pay.

The next thing we did was fasten a fifty pound wooden fish box with a hinged lid on my wagon. Using a bed of crushed ice we would pile our fresh fish in the box. On each side of the box we painted "FISH". We were now ready to go into business. Our plan was to sell door-to-door once a week on Thursday. With nice walleye pike along with a few saugers and perch, we pulled our wagon down every street in Warroad knocking at every door in town. I do not know if we were good salesmen or not, but we sold out our entire stock in no time. I think our low

## Fish Peddlers and Lamplighters

prices did the trick because all of a sudden we had more money than either one of us ever dreamed of.

Not only private homes were buying, but Art Norman's cafe placed a ten pound order for each Thursday. We decided to invest in a rowboat with the idea of netting some of our own fish. It was an old rowboat when we started, but after days of work we rebuilt it and finished the job off with a coat of paint.

The first snag we ran into was brother Dorrance. He said, "Wait a minute, you guys. You are using up so many fish our income is decreasing while yours is increasing." Unable to buy our fish and still sell them at bargain prices, our fish route ended. We did have a nice rowboat and tried gillnetting our own fish by rowing up the Warroad River three miles to "The Forks." Camping out there for two days we did not catch one fish. That was probably a good thing because we quit before the game warden caught us.

My next adventure in the world of big business was when I signed up for a mail order Shetland Pony Contest. As a contestant I was sent a picture of six beautiful ponies and directed to select the one I wanted to win. My choice was Spotty, a black and white pony with a classy saddle.

The first part of the contest was to write as many 7's, without touching each other, inside a drawing of a race track on a sheet of paper. Using a magnifying glass and sharp pencils, I filled the track with hundreds of tiny 7's. Sending the paper in, I was notified that I had won the pony. I was in a dream world the rest of the day; I could just see the envy of the rest of the kids when I rode Spotty through the town.

However, there was one little catch—I must sell six subscriptions to a magazine before they could ship me my pony. Working hard I sold the subscriptions and sent in the money. I never heard from them again and nobody ever received one issue of that magazine.

Dad was always open-mined about me and my friends using his workshop that we all called the Boat House. It was a large shop located along the Warroad River where he built boats during the winter months. All boats and barges used on Lake of the Woods were designed and built by local boatyards. Dad's was a well equipped shop.

In 1930 we had cold weather in November with little snow so the river was ideal for skating and ice boating. My friend Laurence (Barney) Arnesen and I asked Dad if we could build an ice boat in the shop. He said go ahead and use whatever material we needed. Working hard we built a classy looking ice boat while Barney's folks were busy making the sail for it. Selecting a nice straight spruce tree for the mast, our first problem appeared. We could not fit the mast into its anchor block inside the Boat House. It was cold outside so I came up with a brilliant idea—cut a hole in the Boat House roof so we could stick the mast out through the hole while we fitted it to the ice boat.

We did that and were busy fitting it when the door flew open and it was Dad. Blue eyes flashing he was mad! "What the hell do you guys think you're doing cutting a hole in the roof of my shop?"

Barney and I froze waiting for something terrible to happen. Lighting up his pipe, we noticed his hand shaking when he struck the match and began puffing clouds of blue smoke. Turning, he walked back out the door. Barney and I pulled down the mast and nailed a board over the hole. Years later I never

## Fish Peddlers and Lamplighters 59

failed to look up at that board every time I passed the Boat House.

Swimming, skating, boating on the river was our playground. Only one time did I become frightened enough to think the river might do me in. I was fourteen years old during spring breakup. The river ice had "honey-combed" when the surface water drained down through the ice. When that happens the ice is smooth but perforated with tiny holes—it is dangerous ice.

At school, the "across the river boys", the Starrens, Brewesters, and Gordons, along with others were going to play ball and invited me over to join them after school. Running home to change clothes I decided to take a short cut across the river on the ice, instead of running back uptown and crossing on the railroad bridge. The narrow part of the river was from Moyer's Point (present Bill Marvin home) to the sandbar on the south side. I was making good time when "swish", I was in the water with another thirty feet to go. When you break through honey-comb ice it does not crack, you simply go straight through it making a hole the size of your body.

Too far from home or the Moyer house to cry for help, I never felt so alone or helpless. Struggling to climb back out, soon as my body weight rested on the ice, "swish," down I'd go again.

Kicking and using my fingernails to grip the ice, I worked my way toward shore. It seemed to take forever until my feet touched the sandbar. Mrs. Starren dried my clothes and warmed me up at their house. When I went back home I used the railroad bridge! It was such a foolish thing to do that I never told my parents what had happened.

Fascinated by the boats Dad built, I spent hours watching a boat take shape. It was an all-winter job to handcraft a 30-foot launch. White oak ribs were steam bent to form the rib section. The bow stem was also white oak, handcarved and bolted to the oak keel. The oak stern and bow stem were the key to the size and overall shape of the boat. The cedar or cypress boat planking was the most difficult part of boat construction. Each plank was hand shaped to fit the contour of the hull. The caulking seam was an angle cut, made with a wood plane so there was a wedge-shaped grove between each plank. That grove would be "caulked" with cotton using a caulking wheel. The seam was then filled with red lead using a putty knife. When the caulking and sealing was completed the planking was hand sanded smooth and the entire hull was treated with linseed oil, using rags to rub it in. The vessel was then finished with two or three coats of marine paint. When the vessel was ready to launch, the caulking seams could not be detected. Most of the town folks would turn out for the launching, checking out the new addition to Warroad's fishing fleet.

Power was a converted car engine or a marine engine like Red Wing, Universal, Kermith, Lockwood, and others. Marine engines always were equipped with a single lever reverse gear, much better than the low reverse gear ratio found in car transmissions.

I will never forget when I was eleven years old in the spring of 1928 when Dad finished building his new 30-footer, the *Al's Craft*. It was a beautiful gillnetter with cedar planking, decked over bow, and plywood pilot house. Dad powered it with a new four cylinder Universal engine with water cooled manifolds so the cabin would stay cool.

For the maiden voyage down the Warroad River, I had waited all day for brother Dorrance and Dad to

## Fish Peddlers and Lamplighters 61

make final engine adjustments. They fired her up just before dark and the three of us backed out into the channel and headed down the river towards Lake of the Woods. When Dad moved the throttle to "full speed ahead" the *Al's Craft* seemed to fly over the top of the water. It was the thrill of a lifetime to me. I loved that boat and when she was docked after a day of gillnetting, I would go down and slip into the cabin behind the wheel and pretend I was going out to lift my gillnets.

Whenever we left the dock, Dad always trailed a rope along in the water. In the early 1020's Dad's first boat was a 22-footer named *Vernabelle*. She was short with a wide beam making a good gillnetter. Dad's favorite story about the *Vernabelle* is typical of seafaring tales handed down by fishermen working their fishing hear on Lake of the Woods. His story:

"On the way to lift my gillnets at Buffalo Point, I was bucking a north wind gusting to 30 miles per hour. Leaving the Warroad Harbor at daylight it was normally only a half hour run to where my nets were set. However, bucking such a strong wind it would take me over an hour today. I was alone on board when a huge wave rolled over the front deck breaking the anchor loose, causing it to ship back and forth across the deck. In order to secure it I had to climb out and lash it to the deck cleats. Moving the throttle to slow, I lashed the steering wheel so the boat would hold a straight course while I climbed out on the deck and lashed the anchor. Shimmying back into the cabin, a big wave rolled over the bow washing me into the lake. Unable to swim, I was under water until another wave rolled me to the surface just in time to see the *Vernabelle's* stern sliding past. At the same time I saw the stern tie rope dragging in the water. Catching the rope I was towed along behind struggling to pull myself back on board. Exhausted I inched forward far enough to crawl back on board."

From that time on, until he retired from lake work, Dad always trailed a stern rope in the water, just in case.

When the U.S. Lighthouse Service placed the first navigation aids on Lake of the Woods, Dad became the first Lighthouse Keeper.

The first range lights in the Warroad Harbor were mounted on wood pilings, the short one across from Selvog Fishery (now a Casino) and the tall one was located across the river in the old channel. Equipped with large ground lens the lamps projected a good bright light to bring the boats home at night. Lake of the Woods was now as safe to travel at night as it was in the daytime.

Rowing Dad over to light the range lights was always fun. Each light was a kerosene lamp that was hand lighted and filled full of kerosene each evening. This procedure was repeated every evening all summer long. Dad used a little boat to row to each light carrying a can of kerosene to fill them with. His salary was $30 per month paid by the old Lighthouse Service.

To save rowing to each light, Dad bought the first outboard motor in Warroad. It was a single cylinder, with a knob on the fly wheel used to start it. It did not tilt up and was a direct drive. It did not work out for him because if he could get it started, pieces would fall off into the river. He solved this problem by building a tin pan under the engine. When a part

## Fish Peddlers and Lamplighters 63

fell off it would land in the pan so he could reattach it.

The entrance light was acetylene operated with a pilot light that ignited a flash every four seconds. It was mounted on pilings just outside the breakwater in twenty feet of water. It was called the "blinker" by everyone and is still called that to this day. The new blinker operates on solar power mounted on a plastic buoy instead of piling.

Dad retired from the Lighthouse Service in 1942. I was appointed to succeed him and I retired in 1978 with 36 years of government service. When I retired, instead of three aids, I was handling twenty located in both the Little and Big Traverse. Today we have a high-tech navigation system on Lake of the Woods but very little night traffic to use it since the commercial fishing is gone; and freighters like the *Scout, Resolute, Bert Steele,* and *Keenora* which hauled fish and supplies to the Northwest Angle were displaced by the Angle Road which provided Angle residents with a connecting highway to the rest of the United States.

# 8

# First Airplane Ride

From the beginning and still to this day, the only limitation to man's flight is a source of power to create lift by propelling the aircraft wings through the air. On December 17, 1903, Wilbur Wright made the first successful takeoff and landing in the original Wright Flyer. He and his brother Orville had invented the airplane. We can assume that when the Wright Flyer made that first 100-foot flight, Wilbur Wright hoped the engine would not conk out.

Today's pilots still think the same way. The first successful U.S. aircraft engine developed during World War I was the OX V8 Liberty. This beautiful engine was liquid-cooled with overhead valves and an aluminum block. Used to train American pilots, it powered the Curtis Jenny Biplane. The wooden propeller measured nearly seven feet from tip-to-tip, it was also used to crank the engine. The combat version of the OX Liberty was the V-12 (400 hp) used to power the De Havilland DH-4. It was the

## First Airplane Ride

only World War I combat plane made in America to see action in Europe.

In the 1930's air-cooled radial type engines like the Kiner, Veeley, Wasp, Wright Whirlwind, and others made the OX Liberty obsolete. Problems trying to find a suitable coolant plus the weight per horsepower hastened the demise of the Liberty OX. However, successful liquid cooled aircraft engines are still used today because this type of in-line engine is easy to streamline.

The OX Liberty used a magneto ignition system and was hand cranked. Before starting, the propeller was rotated a half dozen turns to avoid oil locks in the cylinders. The pilot's cockpit check consisted of pumping fuel into the engine with a hand operated "wobble" pump. With limited visibility of the propeller area, the pilot and mechanic used certain verbal commands to make sure neither the mechanic nor a bystander was killed with the propeller.

Before starting, the mechanic checked the wheel chocks to make sure that when it started, the airplane would not run over him. The pilot would shout, "Switch off, choke on." After "turning the prop through", the mechanic would position the propeller crossways waiting for the pilot's command, "Contact." Making sure of his footing the mechanic would grasp the tip of the blade, shout, "All clear" and snap it over compression. This was always a two man job because if the throttle was "cracked" too much the aircraft could jump the chocks and injure the prop man or the run-away plane would scare everybody half to death before the pilot could bring it under control. No brakes contributed to the run-away airplane scenario used in early Hollywood screenplays.

## TIME TO FISH—TIME TO DRY NETS

In 1928 the first airplane that I remember seeing was a Travel Air 2000, powered with an OX 5 Liberty. It was a biplane with two open cockpits. The pilot, Russell Riggs, from Morris, Minnesota, flew from the rear cockpit with the passenger in the front. Goggles, helmet and a warm "flight" jacket were the uniform of the day for the pilots. The tiny windshield gave little protection from the propeller's slip-stream.

Using handbills for promotion he announced a free air show for the last weekend in August, he would then hop Warroad passengers. It was in 1928, just one year before the stock market crash plunged the country into the "dirty thirties". Like other barn-storming pilots Russell was in the entertainment business. Dare-devil flying in the 1920's was very grim. When Harriet Quimby, America's first woman pilot, fell to her death after her airplane overturned from wind gusts, pilots began using seat belts. Without seat belts, stable aircraft, parachutes, and with little training very few pilots survived the early years of flying.

My two ten year old friends, Bob Berglund and Susie Beck, were excited when they showed me the Riggs handbill with the details of his upcoming Warroad visit. Bob was lucky enough to have a subscription to the *American Boy*, a magazine with airplane and other adventure stories. None of us had ever seen an airplane except in the movies or in that magazine. Living next to P.W. Chase, our former school superintendent, Bob had already learned a great deal about airplanes from. Very few people knew P.W. Chase was a World War I fighter pilot. In a dog fight over allied lines he was credited with at least one confirmed kill. He was Warroad's first pilot.

## First Airplane Ride

The children's fare was $2.50 each for two, or $5.00 for three (if they could all squeeze in the front cockpit). Children had to have permission from their parents to go up. The $2.50 fare was a full day's work for a man in 1928, if he could find a job.

None of us had any money so Bob and I turned to helping the commercial fishermen dry their gillnets. The linen or cotton nets were dried and treated at least once a week to keep them from rotting. The nets were reeled up on large wooden net reels that would hold a couple thousand feet of netting.

The squeaking reels always needed somebody to turn them while the gillnets were reeled up to dry. One of us would turn the reel while the other helped the fisherman spread the net. One would hold the lead line while the other held the float line. They paid us 25 to 50¢ apiece for each job so it was not long before we had earned money enough to buy our airplane tickets.

Pilot Riggs did a loop or two and landed north of highway 11 where the old ball park used to be. It was a small field but he glided in for a perfect three point landing. The entire town was lined up watching from the highway ditch when he landed and taxied back to the east end of the field. The first thing that caught my eye was the large disk wheels and tiny tail skid. His mechanic hopped out and began selling tickets while the crowd milled around inspecting Warroad's first airplane.

The three of us trailed around behind him while he grabbed off all the adult sales first. Finally when things slowed down he turned to the three of us and our five bucks disappeared into his pocket. When Bob and I reminisce about that ride, Bob always recalls, "I paid my $2.50, you paid your $2.50, and when we climbed into the cockpit Susie climbed in with us and rode for free!" We never have figured out how she worked that scam... We were not only crowded but we could not see out because of our size. Even standing up it was hard to see the ground until he banked making a turn. It was a short but memorable ride that is still just as vivid to Bob and I as it was sixty-six years ago.

Russell Riggs was to become an airline pilot. Flying a Lockheed Orion in 1949 he was killed as the result of a crash landing during a rain squall in Tennessee.

In 1929, flight instructor Art Foster from Detroit Lakes flew his new biplane to Warroad for a visit with his father-in-law, Joe Holland, proprietor of Joe Holland's Beer Parlor. He landed on the Cherne farm south of the Warroad River. Art and his airplane were the main topic of conversation around Warroad while the whole town waited for the weekend and his promised air show.

Dad and I were watching from our yard, on the north side of the river, when the graceful "bird" began its slow climb for an altitude of twenty-five hundred to three thousand feet high. Art did a couple of loops, recovered and probably planned a tailspin when the biplane began a graceful spiral towards the ground. Dad said, "I wish I was up there riding with him." When it disappeared behind a grove of trees Dad and I raced to our rowboat and rowed as fast as we could, across the river to the Cherne farm.

Art was in a fatal "flat spin" (modern aircraft do not flat spin.) He was doing the only thing he could do to recover, giving the engine spurts of power. Arriving at the crash scene, Dad and other men worked to get him free before the plane caught fire. It had hit the ground in a nose-down belly landing with the engine buried in the mud. The impact had

## First Airplane Ride 69

drove the pilot into the tail section, probably saving his life. He was taken to the hospital with facial injuries. The plane suffered the worst damage from people climbing up on the wing to see the bloody cockpit. Art Foster was later killed during World War II as an ambulance driver in Africa.

Unable to buy an airplane, Erling Mickelson of Roseau built one and powered it with a Model A Ford car engine. His mechanic was a machinist by the name of Jensen. Jensen used a converted Ford Model A to power a windsled he built for "Skinny" Springsteel when he lived on Springsteel's Island. He was a natural choice to convert another Ford engine for Erling's single seated monoplane.

Every day Bob and I would rush over to the Ford garage to see if the plane was ready to fly. When the big day arrived we followed the plane while it was towed to a nearby pasture. Erling roared back and forth across the field but could not get airborne. It turned out that the wing's angle of attack was negative. The hickory axe handles supporting the parasol wing were of the wrong length. He washed out the plane on a later attempt. Erling became a flight instructor in Roseau, but not in a home-built airplane.

The first pilot to operate a successful flying service in Warroad was Roy Duggan in 1933 when he was hired by entrepreneur George Arnold to fly his Curtis Robin. Experienced and able to fly anything, Roy was the most able and successful bush pilot to ever fly the big lake. Roy left Warroad to become an Air Force flight instructor in 1939 and ended his career flying DC'3s to Alaska.

In the late 1930's I bought my first flight instruction time from Roy Duggan. The only aircraft he had for instruction was a Savolia Machetti amphibian powered with a 125 hp Kiner five cylinder radial. He flew the plane here from Minneapolis for use as passenger and emergency flights between here and the Northwest Angle. It could carry two passengers and was able to land on either land or water.

At the time, Roy was chief pilot and Clarence Selvog was co-pilot for Hans Selvog's single engine Bellanca, powered with a 420 hp Wasp radial. It was a beautiful airplane equipped with floats for summer and skis for winter. With no connecting road to the Northwest Angle, Roy and Clarence made regular scheduled trips in both the winter and summer.

The mail was hauled by them in the winter and by captain Fay Young on the good ship *Resolute* in the summer. Able to haul enormous loads, the Bellanca was the first successful airplane to operate out of Warroad until Don Hanson and Swede Carlson began flying the new Cessnas in the 1950's. Every Christmas, Roy would make all the city newspapers when he flew Santa Claus into American Point. Before Alaska, American Point was the most northern point of the United States, so it was the first U.S. stop for Santa.

Roy's Savoia Machette was a amphibian and one of the most unusual airplanes to commercially fly Lake of the Woods. It was a biplane with the lower wing only a couple of feet from the water with a small pontoon under each wing tip. On land based biplanes when the lower wing tip hits the ground while landing it was called a "ground loop". In this airplane it would "water loop" if you hooked a wing in the water.

The wooden prop on the Kiner was also the starter. It was a little tricky to crank it by hand while standing on the tiny deck just ahead of the cockpit. Another problem was oil leaks flying back on the cockpit so you wore a white smock and gog-

## First Airplane Ride 71

gles to protect your clothes. Flying the Machette was like sitting on a case of eggs, you moved the controls very gingerly, even shifting your body weight was done with care. This airplane would stall out if the pilot tried a steep-turning bank. So turning was a very gentle maneuver tracing a huge circle in the sky. Not a good student trainer, it was a flying experience no pilot would ever forget.

Roy found a Taylor Craft that was for sale near Grand Forks. Powered with a 40 hp Continental with single ignition, the asking price was $500. The price fit my budget so I bought it. It was a delightful little airplane with side-by-side seating and wheel control instead of a stick. The wooden prop was stamped, "Do not exceed 2450 rpm." The gasoline tank (6 gallons) was located just ahead of the windshield where a tiny rod passed through the tank filler cap. The end of the rod was attached to a cork that floated on top of the gasoline in the tank. It was the most efficient gasoline gauge ever installed in an airplane.

Roy and I flew the "T" Craft to Grand Forks for its annual. While there I received my student permit so I was now ready to become a "hot pilot" with my own airplane.

When Roy and I left Grand Forks to fly to Warroad we hit a service truck on the runway. The accident bent our main wing strut but did not damage the pickup. Roy taxied behind a hanger where we checked the strut out. It was a nasty kink that took the weight of both Roy and I to straighten. Not wishing to get held up at Grand Forks filling out accident reports plus aircraft repair, Roy decided we could fly it to Warroad hoping the damaged strut would hold. The strut was on my side so my job, all the way to Warroad, was to watch for any changes in it. An interesting ride.

Roy's friend, Rudy Billberg, phoned Roy the next day. There was a job waiting for him in Duluth instructing college students under the new government training program. Roy left the next day with no time to teach me how to fly my airplane. After he left the first thing I did was to bolt a steel sleeve around the bent strut to reinforce it. The second thing was to order a book out of *Trade-A-Plane* with the title, "How to Fly a Airplane."

Parking my airplane in the Heppner field north of the present Marvin Window plant, my partner Hugh and I began to gain confidence by taxiing around the field. The more I studied my flying book I knew I could solo out. It was the only way I could use my airplane as there were no other pilots in our section of the state. Forest Rising, at Bemidji, was the only pilot close to Warroad.

One evening Hugh and I were taxing around the field when I turned to him, "Hugh, hop out because I am going to take this airplane around once."

He said, "No way. I'm going with you."

Bouncing across the field we lurched into the air just before reaching the railroad track. Circling town, cars started towards the field thinking a pilot was looking for a place to land. Taking a long approach I came in over Springsteel Island and lined up for my landing. I had two problems that I did not correct: I was coming in too fast and I was short of the field. I just had time to turn to Hugh and say, "Hugh, I am going to crack her up." At the same time I whip-stalled her into a cluster of willows on the lakeshore bog. We climbed out and inspected the plane for damage. Finding only a little fabric tear we repaired her with adhesive tape, pushing the

## First Airplane Ride 73

airplane back out on the field and went for another ride. I had finally "soloed out!"

I made a dramatic rescue from Angle Inlet that winter when ten year old Eleanor Goulet was in serious condition with influenza. With no road there was only one channel of communication from the Angle to Warroad and that was by Alvin Hanson, amateur radio operator and Elmer Carlson, amateur operator here. Unable to make contact in Warroad, Jimmy Gibbons, a guide of Angle Inlet, made a record trip to Warroad. Traveling over 18 inches of loose snow he went 41 miles over an unbroken trail in nine and a half hours on his homemade snowshoes. Running most of the way, his average speed of nearly four and a half miles per hour. This is a Minnesota record that, if recorded, would still stand today.

I left Warroad at once and brought the girl to the Warroad Hospital in my plane. Jimmy Gibbon's heroic effort received national news coverage from the Associated Press through our local correspondent, Mrs. Dick Willems. The news media called me a "Mercy Pilot."

***Top:*** Dorrance H. Johnston in Life Scout uniform holding our pony, Nancy. She was what we used to call an Indian Pony, with a long tail. She was beautiful to ride except one time when I was swinging into the saddle, before I was seated, she ran under my mother's clothes line. She stopped and waited for me to get up. Picture taken down Lake Street. The Bleven's house is in the background.
***Bottom:*** The little lapstrake launch that Dad built for brother Dorrance. It was a delightful little boat with varnished oak seats and a tiny one cylinder marine engine. Hand cranked it had no forward or reverse gear box. It was primed by using a tiny priming cup that we squirted full of gasoline before cranking it. Picture taken in the 1920s with Dorrance at the wheel and sister Vernabelle and me in the back seat.   Photos, Margaret Marvin.

*Top:* Pilot Roy Duggan, 1935, standing on the floats of the six passenger Travelaire owned by Hans Selvog. Powered with a 450 h.p. Wasp radial, it was an excellent float airplane that could carry a ton of freight. His co-pilot was Clarence Selvog. Contracting out to the Superior National Forest Service for $50.00 per hour plus expenses, they fought forest fires for part of the summer of 1936. Engine failure on that job forced Roy to make a landing in a desolate and inaccessible small lake. CCC (Civilian Conservation Corps) men carried a new engine through the swamp suspended on two poles. Roy said, "The Travelaire was a great airplane but a gas guzzler!"

*Bottom:* Ford Trimotor, 1930's, landed at Roseau. The whole town turned out to see it. Photos, Hal Bakke.

*Top:* Bush Pilot Rudy Billberg standing by the Travelaire. Rudy was George Arnold's private pilot flying fish to George's fish stores. He also hauled the mail for Captain Fay Young in the 1930's. Most of Rudy's career was spent as a bush pilot in Alaska. His book, *In the Shadow of Eagles*, is a must for all aviation buffs. Billberg, Duggan, and Klimek were truly the pioneer bush pilots of Lake of the Woods. *Bottom:* Pilot Roy Duggan and Clarence Selvog holding a huge timber wolf that they shot from their plane. A big timber could measure 11 feet from tip of tail to nose when skinned. The county paid a bounty of $25 for timber wolves. With airplanes, they were soon decimated. Photos, Hal Bakke.

*Top:* A 1936 photo of bush pilot, Roy Duggan. Roy's special passenger was a goat. Her milk was needed to save the life of a sick girl in the Northwest Angle. This 1936 picture received nation-wide publicity when it was circulated by the UPS. They called it a "mercy flight." In 1939 Pilot Duggan left Warroad to instruct Air Force pilots. When he left, my 40 h.p. Taylorcraft was the only airplane in our area. When Roy left I soloed out myself.

*Bottom:* Roy Duggan's Savoia-Machetti amphibian he used for emergency flights from Warroad to the Northwest Angle. It carried three passengers and was powered with a 125 h.p. Kiner five cylinder radial. The pilot and passengers wore a helmet, goggles, and a smock to shield them from the oil leaks. Photos, Hal Bakke.

Martin Erickson and I in the late 40's. Martin's Cub Coupe was a classy airplane.

# 9

## Home Ice Delivery—Billy Booze

For fifty years numerous ice houses were scattered along the banks of the Warroad River, and for that matter, all around Lake of the Woods. The ice was harvested in December and January from the Warroad River or Lake of the Woods when it was two feet thick. Each ice cake was two feet by four feet square and weighed 700 to 800 pounds. The Lake of the Woods commercial fishery was big business using up tons of ice during the fishing season.

Every day the fishing fleet loaded up ice to take out on the lake to preserve their day's catch. As a rule of thumb, so much ice melted in the boats that they had to carry two or three pounds of ice for each pound of fish they caught. Ice was the life blood that kept the fisheries going. After the fish were unloaded at Booth or Selvog Fisheries, more ice was used to pack and ship them to the fresh fish markets in Chicago and New York.

In Warroad the Booth Fisheries operation was a huge complex, consisting of fish house, freezers, ice house, docks, and office building. The Booth Fish

Company was a Canadian Corporation with the Warroad branch managed by Bert Steele. Their ice house was a huge wood frame building using 10-inch wide planks for the open wall studding. The ice cakes were stacked up in tiers against the wall studding. Towards spring when "the sawdust was put up," it was poured between the studding for wall insulation, then the top of the ice was covered with another foot or so of sawdust. The sawdust was an efficient insulation preserving the ice all summer long.

The first thing to do if you were "putting up ice" was to mark the size of your ice field and scrape the snow off. Next, mark out a square field so the ice cakes would all be the same size. The ice plow used to cut the ice looked something like the old single bottom horse plow. It was supported in an upright position by the operator, holding on to a handle with each hand while the horse reins hung around his neck. A row of steel cutting blades replaced the curved mold-board, allowing it to cut a straight line a few inches deep each time it was pulled along the top of the ice by the horses, or in later years by a truck. The operator was always careful not to cut all the way through to the water. If that happened, the ice field would be destroyed by flooding.

Each day only the amount of blocks to be put up that day were split loose by striking the plowed cut with a wedge-shaped splitting bar. If done right, the ice split off into nice square cakes. The cakes were then floated to the channel leading to the ice chutes, where the "jack man" positioned the heavy iron jack across the end of the ice cake. Using a pulley system, a cable was fastened to the jack then through an anchor pulley located at the top of the ice chutes. The cable was then strung through a pulley attached to a "dead man" on the ground and was then hitched to a team of horses.

With the horses pulling on the cable, the cake of ice would begin its slow journey up the ice chute to its highest point. From there it would slide down the chutes into the house smashing anything in its way, including a worker's leg now and then. The ice house crew waiting to intercept it used ice tongs, peaveys (a leverage tool), ice shavers, and pry bars to spot it in place. The trick was to keep the wet cake moving—if it stopped it would freeze down.

Another important tool was the hand saw. This saw was five to six feet long, with large coarse teeth. While cutting ice the operator did not dare to stop cutting unless he pulled the saw out of the ice. If he did not do this the saw blade would freeze in and have to be chiseled out. After the ice houses in Warroad were all filled up, Booth Fishery crews left for across the lake. Foremen for the Booth crews were Erick Starren, Art Fish, and John Fealy. Marvin French was the cook, while the three Saurdiff boys, Wilford, Laurence and Ted, handled the horses. George Boucha remembers working for Booth at the Haas Island pound net station in the summer and on the 1929 and 1930 winter ice crew.

According to George, "We would leave Warroad with three teams of horses pulling bobsleds. Each sled had a caboose, heated with an "airtight" wood stove on the front half of the sled. Under the front caboose window, a narrow slot allowed the driver to handle his team's reins. We would go to the twin Canadian islands first, Bigsby and then Haas. After we finished in Canada, we would fill the Booth ice houses on Oak and Garden islands. While on the job, we lived in the company bunk houses on a company living allowance of $55 per month and wages of $1 per day. Sometimes it would be February before we made it back to Warroad."

In the spring, sawdust crews would first have to cut through a foot of frozen sawdust on the outside of the cone-shaped pile. On the inside of the pile sometimes the sawdust would "heat" emitting a tiny spiral of pale vapor all winter long. Using a large hopper, the sawdust would be hoisted to the top of the ice house by a simple pulley system. A horse was used to pull the loaded hopper up where men with scoop shovels spread it around until the ice was covered with a good layer of sawdust.

In the late 1920's, the ice-making machine was invented and the ice harvesting began going the way of the dinosaur. However, ice from the lake was still used by Booth and Selvog Fish Houses up into the late 1950's in Warroad.

On Lake of the Woods, commercial fisherman Ed Vickaryous was the last one to harvest ice in 1974 at Hay Island. Even then things were beginning to change with a pickup truck replacing the horse. When they were running three fishing outfits out of the Hay Island fishery they used up to three tons of ice per day. With over fifty commercial fishermen fishing on Canadian and American waters, it is estimated that 20,000 tons of ice were "put up" in the dozens of ice houses around the lake. Other uses were by railroads for refrigerator express cars, hotels, restaurants, butcher shops, dairy farmers and homes. The first air conditioned railroad coaches were introduced in Canada by packing a metal compartment under the floor full of ice.

The ice for home delivery was harvested three miles out in deep water where there was no pollution and the ice could be used for drinking water. Archie Dumais was Warroad's ice man back in 1926. For

## Home Ice Delivery—Billy Booze

$1.50 a month, he delivered blue, clean ice to your home every day. The ice was washed and delivered on a horse drawn wagon. On a hot day, forty per cent of it would melt before he finished his route. Weighing between twenty-five and fifty pounds, the cakes were smooth and clear, not all frosted up like refrigerator cubes. After placing the block of ice in your icebox, he would usually check the drain pan (it caught the ice water caused by the melting ice) under the icebox to see if it should be emptied.

Using ice tongs, the iceman would sling the ice block on his back, then carry it into the home. His trademark was the rubber apron he wore on his back to keep from getting wet.

We used to chase the ice wagon, as the horses lumbered down the street with ice water dribbling from the wagon. When Archie stopped, we picked up ice chunks to suck on. The ice chips were a pure, tasty candy to us. Archie didn't mind a bit.

The ice house at Billy Booze's fishery on Oak Island played a part in the only Treasury Department raid ever carried out during prohibition by U.S. "Revenuer" agents in the Northwest Angle. Billy was a commercial fishermen that supplemented his income by supplying the local trade with the "best whiskey money can buy." He distilled the booze on a remote island, then hauled the liquor to Oak Island for aging over winter.

On a cold January day in 1930, Billy could not believe it when he counted seven men walking up the path to his house. Husky-looking fellows wearing felt hats, topcoats and business suits, they looked so out of place on Oak Island that Billy wondered if they came from the planet Mars. They certainly did not look like any of his customers, most of whom bundled up in warm fur coats, and kept their feet warm wearing Indian moccasins made out of moose skin.

He soon found out their mission when they showed him a search warrant and a complaint signed by two of his best customers charging him with the illegal distilling of alcohol and selling liquor to the Indians. The men had driven from Warroad, over the ice, to Oak Island on a plowed road used by Art Zippel to haul winter caught fish into Warroad. Apparently their boss in Minneapolis forgot to tell them that a thirty-five mile trip across the ice on Lake of the Woods was a good way to freeze to death in case of a blizzard or breakdown.

They left no stone unturned searching every corner of his home with a professionalism that left the amused locals shaking their heads in disbelief. Coming up empty handed, the exasperated agent in charge finally accosted Billy, "Where have you hidden it? We know it's here."

Billy said, "All I have is a bottle of Canadian Rye, used for medicinal purposes only." Billy continued, "Perhaps you would like a drink to help keep you warm on the long trip back to Warroad."

When Billy finished telling me the story, I asked, "Where was the booze hidden?"

He replied, "Under the sawdust pile, where it was stored in oak kegs to mature and age for the summer trade."

Commercial Fisherman Ed Vickaryous was the last one to put up ice in U.S. waters on Lake of the Woods. His Hay Island fishery was on the Canadian and U.S. border. Ed was the most colorful fisherman we had. In this 1974 picture Ed is working the channel. Note the long ice chutes going up to the ice house; as each tier of ice was packed the chute would be raised up the thickness of the ice and a new tier started. Six or seven tiers was about all a ice house could hold. Either horses or a truck pulled the ice up the chute. Each cake of ice weighted about 800 pounds so if one broke loose and sailed back down the chute, nothing could stop it.

# 10

## The Mighty *Scout*

Technically, the *Scout* was a ship. A ship is a larger craft, one that requires the use of a dry dock. The only one large enough to handle her was in Kenora, on the Canadian side of Lake of the Woods.

The *Scout* was commissioned by the Booth Fishery Company in the year 1923 with its home port Warroad, Minnesota. She was a documented vessel registered at 92 tons and was designed as a freighter with staterooms for eleven first class passengers. As a motor ship, she was licensed to carry 125 passengers.

When her new Diesel engine arrived on a railroad flat car, it had traveled a long ways from the Kalenberg factory in Germany. It had only been ten years since the death of the German inventor, Rudolf Diesel. This new type of internal combustion engine burned fuel oil; the ignition is brought about by heat resulting from air compression, instead of by electric spark as in a gasoline engine. So the *Scout*,

## The Mighty *Scout*

with her new 120 horse power Diesel engine, utilized the brand-new marine technology that replaced the steam engine.

The *Scout* was a sturdy craft, a wood hull with two-inch thick planking. With a length of 78-feet and a 20-foot beam, her "high board" (the distance from the main deck to the waterline) created a silhouette on the horizon that could be seen for miles on the lake. With steel sheeting from the waterline down, she was an excellent ice breaker smashing through four inches of ice. The rest of the fishing fleet would follow her out of the harbor to take advantage of the late fall fishing run.

From midsection forward, the deck could hold four automobiles. With no roads from here to Kenora, the Canadians brought their automobiles along with them so they could drive to Winnipeg from Warroad. This vessel, on one single trip to her home port, sailed across Lake of the Woods with the monumental load of fifty thousand pounds of fish. That 25 ton load will stand as the single largest load of fish ever carried across the lake. A swinging boom hoist loaded and unloaded the fish through deck hatches located on the forward deck.

All fish were packed fresh in one hundred pound wooden fish boxes, with a layer of ice on the bottom and top. To get the fish and freight unloaded in Warroad, uptown help was hired to unload, sometimes they would work all night. None of the fish were frozen so they were graded, repacked in ice, then loaded on railroad express cars for the fresh water fish markets in Chicago and New York.

The round-trip passenger fare to Kenora was $3 per person. To bring your car along from Kenora, cost $12.50 if it was a light Model T Ford. The cost for a big heavy touring limousine could cost up to $35.

It was a glorious day when the majestic *Scout* sailed out of the Warroad Harbor on her maiden voyage. Captain Erick Starren stood in front of the big steering wheel, handmade, three feet in diameter with spokes providing oak handles all around the wheel. Two small cables with wood handles were suspended from pulleys secured to the ceiling of the pilothouse and operated the bells. The small bell would ring the engineer—one jingle ahead, two reverse, and three slow. The other was called the jiggler bell used after leaving the pier and was jiggled for full speed ahead.

The pilot house was twenty feet above the waterline and was large enough to include the captain's private cabin. Captain Starren looked out over the big open deck, reached up and gave one jingle on the small bell, engineer John Vog slammed the big reverse gear into forward, the *Scout* headed down the Warroad River on her maiden voyage. First mate Louie Carom was at his station in the pilothouse watching as she cleared the dock. On the main deck Lawrence Saurdiff, deck hand, coiled up the mooring lines.

That first year Lawrence had worked less than three months when first mate Caron decided to celebrate Dominion Day. The July 1st holiday is when Canadians celebrate the proclamation in 1867 of the establishment of the Dominion of Canada. It was apparently some celebration because the first mate did not report back to the *Scout* until July 4th. Captain Starren met him at the gang plank and said, "You're fired," turned to Lawrence and said, "You're the new first mate." With that promotion,

# The Mighty *Scout*

Lawrence began his career on Lake of the Woods that was to span five decades, a number of years as captain of the *Scout* after Erick Starren retired.

In the galley, ship's cook Art Grundman was busy preparing dinner for the crew and passengers. Art was, without a doubt, the best cook on the lake. He baked pie the old-fashioned way. A big friendly man, his cooking was always remembered if you were a passenger on the *Scout*. Three hours out of Warroad they docked at Garden Island. That was a Booth Fishery station that boasted a 70-foot long dock with a huge ice house, fishery and bunk house for the fishermen stationed there. The crew and company dignitaries celebrated that first trip with a sumptuous meal served by cook Grundman while the *Scout* was tied up at the dock.

The sixth crew member was the custom officer Bill Hail. Over 50% of the fish loaded on the *Scout* came from Canadian waters so with officer Hail on board, all passengers and freight were cleared for entry into the U.S. He was also in charge of all ship's records and noted that at 150 gallons of fuel per round trip to Kenora, it cost $18 to make the trip, at 12¢ per gallon.

In the 1940's the *Scout* started to stumble with the demise of the commercial fishing industry caused by various political factors. The first to go was the bullhead fishery located in Northwest Angle Inlet. This was the beginning of the end for the American Point complex that included the sawmill, post office, and general store. Moose Bay, Oak Island, and the Little Traverse were soon to follow.

With increased activity in resort development along with the loss of the island fisheries there was not enough freight to support the *Scout* so the Booth Fishery placed her in mothballs. She ended up behind a tow rope being snaked across the lake to Stony Point, beached on the bar, to be used as a duck hunting camp. A few years later she caught fire and burned to the waterline. Her keel is still buried in the muskeg out there. For a number of years, her charred skeleton could be seen from the lake. A bony framework sticking out of the water, a symbol of the commercial utilization of Lake of the Woods. It played a role, a part of the overall scheme of things that moved Warroad out of the pioneer days when the lake was the reason that there was a town here.

The *Scout* was still running in 1939 when, as a young commercial fishermen, I followed her out of the Warroad Harbor in a thick, soupy fog. It was a dead calm day before sunrise, cold enough to cap the river with one inch of clear, blue ice. There was not even a tiny ripple on the water. The lake was like a piece of glass that had neither a beginning nor an end. The fog acted lazy as it started to swirl, collecting into thick banks when the sun peeked over the horizon starting to warm it up. With one hour of running time, the sun was doing its job. I now had a few feet of visibility. Slowing down to an idle, I opened the cabin window, checked my watch, one hour and ten minutes, the compass was steady, I should see my net buoy any second now. I was straining my eyes, looking, when there was the *Scout* dead ahead!

I knew her course was Oak Island so she should have been about five miles south of Stony Point, instead of on a collision course with Gull Rock.

"I must head her off, she is lost. My God, in a few minutes she will hit Gull Rock and sink to the bottom." I closed my eyes for a moment, to rest them, then looked again. "There is no wake behind her. Why can I not hear the loud exhaust? Oh, no! I am going to ram her!" But right before my eyes, she sailed off from the water and into the sky. That optical illusion was a seagull, a hallucination, only a mirage. I think she is still sailing up there, I know she is...

Inside the Booth Fishery where the fish were graded, prepared for market, and shipped out to the fresh fish markets in Chicago and New York city. Expert crews worked, sometimes around the clock, to move the fresh fish to the market before they spoiled. Left is Leon Whilsee, right is Art Fish. In the foreground is the cleaning tables and scale where the fish were dressed. This fish house was so large it had three cleaning tables. Twenty to thirty men worked seven days a week during the fishing season. Photo, Warroad Heritage Center.

***Top:*** The mighty *Scout* was commissioned in 1923 by the Booth Fishery Co. registered at 92 tons, she was licensed to carry 125 passengers. Her one trip load of 50,000 pounds of fish from the Northwest Angle to her home port of Warroad is a record that will stand forever. The *Scout* was an imposing example of the Booth Fishery's fleet of vessels.
***Bottom:*** The *Keenora*, 100 feet long, was the largest steamship to ever sail Lake of the Woods. Her home port was Kenora.

***Top:*** The steam tug *Isobel* docked alongside the fish barge *Rose M.* at the Booth Fishery dock in Warroad. A few years later the *Rose M.* was converted into a diesel vessel called the *Scout*. The *Scout* was owned by the Booth Fishery Company with Captain Erick Starren as captain.
***Bottom:*** The U.S. Corps of Engineers *Lakewood*. Used to pull the *Big Traverse* dredge. Its captain was Trevor Gerry. It was one of the most beautiful boats to sail Lake of the Woods. Photos, Warroad Heritage Center.

*Top:* The Isobel at the Booth Fishery in Warroad. A powerful tug, she was powered with a steam engine and burned wood. Used to tow fish barges and timber booms to Warroad and Baudette, she was the last steam tug to operate in U.S. waters on Lake of the Woods. Her last owner was Leo Welsh who owned the Welsh Timber Company of Warroad. Probably about 1915. Photo, Warroad Heritage Center.

*Bottom:* Spooner, Minnesota, home of the S.M. mills. A mill of this size could produce five million feet of lumber per annum. It was estimated that six million feet of logs were lost from log booms and scattered over Lake of the Woods.

*Top:* The steam tug *Na-Ma-Puk* owned by the Armstrong Trading Company. She sank to the bottom in 40 feet of water three miles off of Oak Island, September 3, 1909. She was towing a barge full of fish in heavy sea. The crew of seven men and two passengers abandoned the ship and managed to board the fish barge. The barge drifted with its ship-wrecked crew to the mouth of the Rainy River where they were rescued.
*Bottom*: Captain Fay Young's first vessel, the *Nina*. She was used to haul freight and passengers to the Northwest Angle. Taken in the early 1900's. Photos, Warroad Heritage Center.

Captain Fay Young's fleet, the *Resolute* and the *Nina*, docked in Warroad. Top picture from the old watertower. Top photo, Warroad Heritage Center.

# 11

## Winter Commercial Fishing and Slush

Commercial fishing on Lake of the Woods, through the ice, began in the early 1900's. In the beginning nets were set close to the home grounds of the fisherman so he could use a hand-sled and walk out to lift his nets. This began to change when the commercial value of their catch encouraged them to range away from the shoreline and venture out into "deep water".

Along with the increased commercial value of the catch another problem confronted the fishermen. Transportation to and from their nets, over drifting snow, rough ice, and open compression ridges, started a search for ways to replace the handsled.

The logical choice was the horse, however, deep snow, slush, and wind chill that reached 60 to 70 degrees below zero exhausted the best horses. Most teamsters would never use their horses on the lake during the winter.

The next choice was the automobile. It was fast when the going was good, but it too, was helpless in deep snow and slush. With snowplows attached (when cars became powerful enough to push them) they were more efficient but unable to handle hard lake drifts or slush holes. Even to this day powerful automobiles are not the answer to winter travel on the big lake. Track machines that ride on top of the snow, and in some cases will carry up over slush beds, are successful vehicles used today for sport fishing.

Another problem with cars were break downs. They would not stand up under the cold and constant wear-and-tear caused by the use of tire-chains day after day.

During the 1930 winter, Dad, brother Dorrance, and Moose Hilborne, were fishing their gillnets about twelve miles out from Warroad. Fishing was good and they were getting along fine using a Dodge Coupe with a powerful transmission and over-sized tires.

The "good days" ended when a heavy snowfall covered the ice with two foot of snow creating ideal slush conditions. The weight of the snow caused the ice to sag and flood when water squirted up through cracks covering the ice with lake water. The deep snow then insulated the water so it did not freeze up again.

Soon as the snowfall ended, Dad, Dorrance, and Moose fired up the old Dodge, ready to lift their nets before the new snow became drifted into hard drifts, making car travel impossible. They had no trouble driving out to their nets through the loose snow. It was dark before they finished lifting their nets and loaded up the fish for the trip home.

When the sun disappeared, it turned bitter cold. The north wind blew the loose snow in an endless, rolling sheet of white, making you became mesmerized and disoriented. There was neither a begin-

## Winter Commercial Fishing and Slush

ning nor an end. The drifting snow was formidable with the only guiding light miles away on the town water tower.

With Dorrance at the wheel, they were making good time until the Dodge dropped into a deep slush hole. When they abandoned the old Dodge, the water, snow, and cold weather made the slush thick and heavy, like walking in fresh concrete. Still a long way from home, they prepared to walk to Warroad. It would be a formidable trip in the deep snow and slush with the wind chill fifty below zero. Guided by the water tower light, they began the long walk back home to Warroad. The other alternative was to spend the night there with no shelter or fire to keep them warm.

It was bitter cold by now, so cold that when they lifted their feet for another step forward the wet boot would crust up with a thin layer of ice. With each step, the ice became thicker until the boot was so heavy they would have to stop and pound off the ice so they could continue to walk. Moose, at 250 pounds, was having the most trouble walking. Dad and Dorrance realized the danger when Moose cried out, "I'm all in, I cannot take another step. I must lay down and rest."

Dad cried, "No! No! If you lay down in this slush you will die, we will never be able to get you on your feet again." Rushing to his side, they stopped him from going down, knowing very well he was sinking into a profound lethargy and that his chance of survival in this present condition was nil. The only thing they could think of was to jar him back to reality by shouting at him, "Moose! Snap out of it, if you go to sleep you will die out here. If you go down, we will never be able to get you to your feet again. Remember that teamster that tried freighting from the Northwest Angle a few years ago? His team dropped into a slush hole in the middle of the night, it was cold like it is tonight. As the horses waded through the water, their hoofs iced down, forming huge ice tubs on each foot. The tired horses dropped into the slush, unable to take another step. The teamster had to shoot them. Moose! You must continue! Snap out of it! Let's make it home."

When Dad told me the story he said, "The only thing that seemed alive was the Warroad water tower light shining in the dark, it gave all of us hope. Moose snapped out of his exhaustion and broke trail for Dorrance and I until we reached the edge of the slush bed and found solid ice to walk on. It was near daylight when we reached home."

# 12

## Little Mike's Death—Lake Casualties

After the Canadian Pacific Railroad linked up to Warroad in the early 1900's, Warroad became the center of the commercial fishing industry on Lake of the Woods. The early "lake people" were attracted by thousands of acres of virgin timber that lined the shores of Lake of the Woods, others settled around the lake shore to become commercial fishermen. The water was their means of transportation.

Warroad was a melting pot for a mixed population of every nationality. They were not farmers because Lake of the Woods was surrounded by swamps and peat bogs until later on when huge floating dredges ditched them. Living alone or in small settlements on fishing stations located on Stony Point, Oak Island, Rainy River, Zippel Bay, Long Point, Rocky Point, Willow Creek, Warroad River, Elm Point, Oak Island, and Springsteel Island, they became independent thinkers, surviving under difficult conditions.

Sturgeon, white fish, and goldeyes were their main commercial catch. The so called "game fish", of today were not plentiful. In the last 100 years there was has been a drastic change in the fish population of Lake of the Woods. One wonders what changes the next 100 years will bring.

These sturdy lake people loved the lake and always thought of it as feminine (she's calm, she's rough, etc.) They knew she could do wild and wicked things but, if she did, they knew she could not help it. She would take family members or friends away from them, but they never blamed the lake. They knew everyday is a new day, that to be a survivor in this wild and untamed land you must be lucky, that without luck you might not return from a days fishing. If that happened to you, the unknown tale would remain her secret, buried under the sandbars and beneath the waves forever.

The most common means of early lake transportation was the Indian's invention, the birchbark canoe. The white man never did develop the sense of balance and skill needed to use this invention. On the other hand, the Indians were at home in their canoe, using it for transportation, to hunt, fish, harvest wild rice, and trap muskrat, beaver, and mink. They would paddle from Rat Portage (Kenora) to Warroad and Rainy River.

The ribs and keel were made out of white cedar bound together with strips of tanned moose and deer skins. When wet, the raw hide would shrink, binding the ribs, keel, and ash stringers together as one unit. Birchbark, peeled from huge trees, was strong and waterproof, it covered the skeleton frame making the canoe watertight and strong.

The birch bark pieces were cemented and bound to the ribs with clear colored pitch collected from

### Little Mike's Death—Lake Casualties 103

the trees. Black tar, depicted by artists, was not used because there was no tar to be found in our forests. Narrow and limber, the canoe was easy to paddle. For the unwary, it was another story, it could flip them upside down into the lake without warning. As a young man hunting ducks at Buffalo Point, I was using one of Tommy Lightning's birch bark canoes when I made the mistake of turning sideways while firing at ducks flying past. Before I knew it, I was in the water looking at my upside down canoe floating away. Clutching my shotgun, I touched lake bottom in only four feet of water and was able to wade to shore, towing the capsized canoe behind me.

When I was two years old my Grandpa's brother, Ferdinand Guhl, walked into open water caused by "putting up ice" at Northwest Fishery. It was pitch-black and bitter cold, the north wind and snow creating a blinding blizzard. He was carrying a packet of mail for Grandpa. The next morning, the mail was the clue to what happened. It had floated on top of the water until it became embedded in ice. Because of that accident, a Minnesota statute was enacted requiring a safety fence around all open ice fields.

In 1933 when I was 16 years old, my friend and neighbor, little Mike Moyer, lost his life while playing on the Garden Island Beach near his Dad's commercial fishing station. He was the youngest of the six Moyer boys and a favorite of everyone. We all looked after him while we were swimming in the Warroad River or playing games like Run Sheep Run, or Anti-I-Over, etc. None of the games seemed the same after he was gone—only The Lake knows what happened. He was playing with his brothers on the sand beach when The Lake reached out and Mike was gone.

## TIME TO FISH—TIME TO DRY NETS

It was my first exposure to death and it still is a vivid memory to me years later. Mike's Dad and brothers brought him back to Warroad in Lew's pound net boat. It was a 30-mile trip from Garden Island to Warroad so, the body was preserved with crushed ice and covered with a tarp in the stern of the boat. All of us Lake Street kids were hushed and some of us cried when the boat pulled into Lew's dock.

After docking, the body was moved into the Moyer fishery where an ice bin was made across the corner of the building to hold the body until burial. Dad helped Lew make a pine coffin on the same bench where fish boxes were built.

As was the custom in those days, someone always stayed with the body to watch over it. When family and friends attended a special prayer service for little Mike that afternoon, I was asked to stay in attendance and guard the body from rodents or other animals that might be attracted to it. Left alone I was suppose to look into the building every few minutes to make sure it was all right. Nothing would have made me peek into that building. When Ed, his oldest brother, returned I ran home and hid in my room. The grief of losing my friend washed over me in waves.

In those days it was the custom to have young friends serve as pallbearers. Three of my friends and I were pallbearers for little Mike. With no handles on the coffin we used a piece of rope under each end to carry it. The hearse was a wagon pulled by a team of horses all decked out in black webbed blankets.

In 1917, Rupert Hilborne was the first Warroad commercial fisherman to lose his life while working nets on the big lake. Each death is surrounded by peculiar circumstances caused by a conjunction of

## Little Mike's Death—Lake Casualties    105

high winds, freezing temperatures, unseaworthy boats, overloading, and other unavoidable conditions. Commercial fishing was a high risk occupation and still is to this day. Rupert was the brother of Clarence (Moose) and Lloyd Hilborne who had moved here from Northhome, Minnesota, to homestead on Stony Creek just two years before. They joined a growing settlement of commercial fishermen making their home on 160 acre tracts of public land called "claims" under the Homestead Act. They must live on their claim for one year. If they complied to all the rules and regulations they were granted free title to the land.

Stony Creek provided an excellent harbor with high banks covered with virgin growth timber. It was a 20-mile long trip, across the open water or ice to Warroad. Transportation was by boat in the summer, and dog sled or walking in the winter.

Rupert was working all alone pulling hoop nets at Stony Point during the fall freeze-up. His boat swamped and Rupert was unable to swim to shore in the freezing water. Clarence and Lloyd proved up their homestead and moved to Warroad after the accident.

In 1926 Ewald Schafer, a 17-year old Warroad boy, drowned while working for his brother-in-law Frontie Parker. Ewald was my brother Dorrance's best friend. A fair complexion along with blonde colored hair he was an attractive young man. He and Frontie were gillnetting near Gull Rock, 14 miles from Warroad. The surface of the lake was flat, except for tiny thermals of hot air rippling the water as they moved along. It was a beautiful morning on Lake of the Woods.

Frontie's launch was a new 36-footer, a beautiful boat that Bess Squires had built for him. Arriving at the nets, Ewald eased the engine out of gear, allowing the boat to slide to a halt while Frontie was pulling on his oilers and rubber boots. Untying the tow line, Frontie climbed into their lifting boat, a 14-foot flat bottom row boat used to handle the gillnets, and rowed over to the up-wind net buoy. Pulling the end of the gill net across the bow of his lifting boat he began picking out the fish. As he pulled along the net, the fish were picked out before the net returned to the water on the other side of the boat.

On that fateful day, fishing was good and Frontie anticipated they would sell at least fifty dollars worth of fish to Warroad's Booth Fishery when they finished lifting.

Concentrating on picking fish Frontie did not look up until reaching the middle of the string of nets. Straightening up he expected to see Ewald waiting in his launch only 500 feet away. But instead the boat was empty and drifting downwind. He could see the net buoy that Ewald was supposed to pickup and secure to the launch while waiting for him. He could not see any sign of Ewald holding on to the buoy or swimming in the water near by. Dropping the net he rowed hard but steadily towards the drifting launch hoping to find Ewald on board. Voices carry very well on the water, yet he had not heard a splash nor a cry for help. Catching up to the launch, it was empty—Ewald had disappeared without a sound.

Why had he not cried for help? When he fell into the water, why did he not hold on to the buoy, until Frontie could row over and pick him up? An experienced "lake man" how did he fall out of the launch on a calm day? Only the lake knows what happened and it can never tell. It was surmised that

## Little Mike's Death—Lake Casualties

Ewald ran up to the buoy a little too fast. When he ran to the stern to pick it up, the momentum of the launch was strong enough to drag him overboard. There is still no answer to the question. Why did he not cry out for help when was in hailing distance from Frontie?

Dad and brother Dorrance found the body in 30 feet of water near the net buoy by dragging a long pipe along the bottom. The pipe had surgeon hooks tied to it at six-inch intervals. The sturgeon hooks were left over from the days when my Grandpa used baited setlines to catch them.

Commercial fisherman Chet Carlquist, was forty years old when he was found dead, all alone, in his boat on the Garden Island Bar. The oldest of two Carlquist boys, he was a prominent Warroad pioneer that developed the Carlquist block that still dominates downtown Warroad. My helper, Bill Growette, and I were lifting gillnets on Archie's Reef when Chet had stopped to visit on his way to his fishing grounds on Garden Island. It was a pleasant summer day with no wind so the lake was smooth as glass. We shared our lunch with him and we waved goodbye to each other when he set his course for Garden Island, 16 miles away. He was loaded with crushed ice in wooden fish boxes.

Two days later, Bill and I heard the sad news that Chet was found dead, sprawled on the floor of his launch with the engine still running. The hull was beached on the shallow sand bar that surrounds Garden Island. It appeared that Chet may have lost consciousness from carbon monoxide fumes caused by a faulty exhaust pipe. Even though it made no sense, I felt there should have been something that I could have done since I was the last one he talked to.

## TIME TO FISH—TIME TO DRY NETS

Young Bob Vickarious was from an old line commercial fishing family. His father, Ed, lived on Oak Island until moving his family to Hay Island. The Vickarous family still owns Hay Island. It is located between Little Oak and Big Island.

Bob was not only a commercial fishermen, he was the owner and operator of an all-steel freighter that hauled freight from Warroad to the Northwest Angle. His first mate was Don Corneliusen. In 1972, he and Don were freighting underwater electrical cable to Oak Island for the Roseau REA. The heavy cable came in huge spools probably six feet in diameter. On this trip the spools were loaded on edge in a row on the cargo deck. Leaving town in the evening their voyage went along smooth until they were 16 miles out, near Archie's Reef. It was not storming but there was a little roll from the breeze that was blowing. Don, in the pilot's cabin felt a little uneasy as their vessel was unsteady. Relieved of the wheel, Don left the cabin to check the cargo out when he was catapulted into the water as their boat rolled upside down.

When he surfaced, Don could see the bottom of the vessel silhouetted with the big Caterpillar diesel engine still spinning the propeller around in thin air.

Swimming over to the lifting boat they were towing, he started up the outboard and began circling the hull looking for Bob. Unable to find him he drove the lifting boat back into Warroad for help. Skin divers later found Bob in the pilot's cabin. It is believed that he was thrown against a bulkhead and knocked unconscious or he would have escaped the accident.

The Scottish poet and novelist Sir Walter Scott, 1771-1832, wrote. "It's not fish ye're buying, its men's lives."

# 13

## Prohibition—Ma & Pa Teachout

**P**olitics has a funny way of tripping people up, but they somehow or other find their way just the same. The "Dirty Thirties" were a combination of politics, greed, and manipulation of the money markets by unscrupulous money lenders. Those years were full of misery and hardship for everyone, especially for the sick and old.

Very few people in Warroad lost any money in the 1929 stock market crash because nobody had any money to invest in it. However, the "Dirty Thirties" reached out and touched everybody. The rich were no longer rich and the poor became paupers supported by meager public funds. This condition changed very little until the outbreak of World War II in 1941.

Weary and discouraged voters elected Franklin Roosevelt to the office of President in 1933. FDR's New Deal would repeal Prohibition, allowing the working man to buy a mug of beer for 5¢. Beer was the poor man's drink, champagne was imbibed only in the movies.

## 110  TIME TO FISH—TIME TO DRY NETS

The public paid 25 to 50¢ to see Hollywood's portrayal of the "good life" where rich, beautiful people descended a spiral staircase in a millionaire's mansion sipping champagne. A gorgeous lady dressed in a formal evening gown was usually a judge's daughter. Instead of wearing her mink coat (if she did we could not see her beautiful figure) she usually was dragging it along on the floor behind her.

FDR's running mate, Cactus Jack Garner, was a wealthy Texan that made no bones about what he thought was needed to straighten out the country: "What this country needs is a good 5¢ cigar." That was Cactus Jack's contribution to FDR's campaign. He knew the working man either chewed tobacco or "rolled their own" from a sack of Duke's Mixture. Garner was a good politician.

FDR's New Deal did help some people but it backfired for Warroad's oldest couple, Ma & Pa Teachout. During Prohibition they generated a little income by selling home brew for 15¢ per bottle. With end of prohibition, that income was gone. Pa, a former commercial fisherman, had moved to Warroad with his wife in 1929 when they could no longer operate their fishery on a tiny island called Teachout's Island in the Little Traverse area of Lake of the Woods. Despite his poor health Pa decided to go back on the lake. His teenage grandson Buddy agreed to help him. They had a rowboat but no money to buy an engine. They rigged up two pair of oars and rowed back and forth to lift their nets every day. Selvog fishery supplied them with nets and the money to pay for the license.

Every morning at daylight, Pa and Buddy's boat was the first out of Warroad harbor. With both of them rowing hard, they moved along at a good clip if they did not have to buck a head on wind. In case of a strong wind, some of us would toss them a line so we could tow them the three miles to their nets down the south shore. They were good fishermen, surprising the rest of us with the amount of fish they caught. Near the end of July, they had saved almost enough money to buy an outboard, when the worse thing that can happen to a fisherman happened to them. The game wardens seized all their nets and convicted them of fishing illegally. Their claim that Pa was fishing "small mesh" meant his nets measured less than the legal four inch required by law. The hefty fine along with the warden's confiscation of their nets and boat eliminated Pa's last chance to make a living. They were out of business.

His life took another turn of events, even worse than losing everything, the judge sentenced him to a jail term, because he had no money to pay his fine. With nobody to take care of her, Ma's health deteriorated enough so she could no longer take care of herself.

She was befriended by her next door neighbors, my brother Dorrance and his wife Eudora. With cold weather in December, they checked on her every day to see if she was all right. On this Christmas morning, they found the fire beginning to flicker in the oil heater used to heat her home. When they checked the outside storage tank, the gauge showed it was empty. The oil heater was going but not for long.

Unable to reach Bill Saurdiff, the delivery man, on the phone, they began driving around town looking for him. When they found him, Bill assured Dorrance he would fill Ma's fuel tank as soon as he finished a few other deliveries.

Bringing a Christmas dinner over to Ma, Dorrance and Eudora found the house was getting cold.

Ma was sitting at the kitchen table with her hands clasped together, her head was bowed, and she was praying, "Dear God, the stove is out of fuel, the house is getting cold. I am all alone, old and sick, with no money to buy fuel. Please help me."

At that instant, the dying fire came to life, They could hear Bill filling the outside tank. Looking up at the bright red glow of fire now burning again, Ma bowed her head and said, "Thank you, Dear God."

Ma and Pa lived to celebrate their fifth wedding anniversary in 1938. Death called Pa in 1942.

Franklin Delano Roosevelt's landslide victory over Herbert Hoover was a victory of the "wets" over the "drys." The voters reaction was: "Who could ask for anything more? A glass of beer and a cigar for 5¢."

The new law repealed prohibition but it provided for each state to go either wet or dry. Minnesota voted wet with a county option decided by popular vote.

Warroad, recognizing the economic value of a wet county to tourism, voted wet while Roseau, and the west section of the county, had enough votes to keep the county dry. Not only was the wet vote a hot issue between Warroad and Roseau, but the Roseau Conservation Club was flexing their new found political muscle by trying to close Lake of the Woods to commercial fishing. These two issues were to become very emotional and highly controversial, causing hard feeling between the two towns. Some of these feelings still exist 60 years later.

At that time there were regular scheduled carriers operating from Warroad to the Northwest Angle and on up to Kenora. Vessels like the *Resolute*, *Scout*, and *Bert Steele* were all registered and docu-

### Prohibition—Ma & Pa Teachout 113

mented according to their tonnage. They were classified under the same rules and regulations as ocean-going vessels. One important distinction that applies to documented vessels is that only Federal officers have any authority to inspect or board the vessel. Using this premise as his legal basis, Warroad's enterprising entrepreneur, George Arnold, conceived a bold and daring scheme: He would build a floating nightclub complete with bar and dance floor.

It would be classified as a documented vessel operating on International Waters. As such it would not be under the jurisdiction of Roseau County laws. By circumventing the Roseau County dry vote, all he would need is a federal liquor stamp. Local authorities would have no legal right to board or interfere with the operation of this vessel. A bold and daring idea that could make George a lot of money.

The Warroad merchants, along with the local residents, had no objection to George's idea of a floating nightclub. Some looked on with amusement, others with anticipation, looking for additional business opportunities in our town. To show support there was a contest to select a name for the new "club". The winning name was "Harbor Lites." The young crowd called it "Do Drop Inn and Stagger Out."

The *Harbor Lites* was built in Warroad, using a huge steel barge for the hull. Completed in 1939, the *Harbor Lites* sported a fancy new bar, booths and tables. There was a little postage-stamp size dance floor and a small landing entrance deck. When it opened its doors for business it was the only saloon in Roseau County that could sell hard liquor. The only competition were beer parlors that sold nonintoxicating beer with an alcohol content of not over 3.2%.

On the advice of his attorney (a Duluth maritime expert), George moved his *Harbor Lites* to the end of Main Street, near uptown Warroad. To board this vessel, the passenger (customer) walked a gangplank with an eight-foot span to reach shore. Apparently there was a legal technicality. The gangplank could not touch land, so each customer had to take a long step to get on board. We could then assume the good ship *Harbor Lites* was legally sailing the high seas on International Waters beyond the long arm of the Roseau County sheriff.

Nobody ever mentioned another technical point: the *Harbor Lites* had neither an engine nor a propeller.

A friend of mine, Jody Norman, was hired as club manager and bartender. Jody had worked the previous summer for me gillnetting, but left commercial fishing for job security on the *Harbor Lites*. He was a good friend, happy-go-lucky, always looking for something to do that might offer a little excitement. Excitement a-plenty was waiting for him on his new job.

The *Harbor Lites* opened with good promotion and no problems from the village constable. Traffic into Warroad virtually tripled overnight. Not only was George Arnold making money "hand over fist" but the whole town was riding on a money roller coaster.

However, the Roseau County Temperance Society, began exerting political pressure on the County Attorney, Bert Hanson. They demanded that he exorcise Roseau County of what was then called the evil spirit "demon rum."

## Prohibition—Ma & Pa Teachout 115

Bert Hanson's dilemma was whether he should raid his own "watering hole" where he and his old Warroad cronies would rehash the "old days." If he did not raid his friend George Arnold's new gold mine, he would take a chance on losing the next election. Bert did what all politicians have always done: sell out friends if it is necessary to keep your job. The *Harbor Lites* was raided with all the liquor on board seized and manager Jody Norman was carted off to the county jail.

Jody was released from jail the next morning and rumors were that all the booze was returned to George when he made a deal with the County Attorney to move the *Harbor Lites* down to the mouth of the Warroad River where it was moored in Lake of the Woods County. That county was "wet" so there was no legal reason to close it.

The *Harbor Lites* was anchored across the Warroad River from the swimming beach so the patrons had to row across the river in a row boat to enjoy all the good things in life that the *Harbor Lites* had to offer.

The most exciting thing that ever happened on board the good ship happened to an attractive young lady from Canada. She and her boy friend Art had spent the afternoon sampling Jody's liquor inventory. They were unaware that the temperature had dropped to zero and frozen a layer of ice across the river. She was dressed for freeze-up weather and looked beautiful in her new fur coat. It was after dark when they decided to leave the *Harbor Lite's* party. When Art opened the door for her, she marched straight out towards the outside deck. Before disappearing she paused for a moment to toss an exuberant, "Good night all" over her shoulder. Reaching the deck, instead of turning and using the gangplank, she plowed straight ahead off of the landing and crashed through the ice to the bottom of the Warroad River. Thrashing around in the water, her boyfriend responded to her cries of "help" by holding his flashlight on her so Jody could reach her with a long pike pole. Everybody was shouting, "Grab it and hang on, we'll get you out!"

When Jody and Art pulled her up on the landing, her beautiful black hair was hanging straight as a stick, with pieces of river ice giving it a jeweled appearance. The matted fur coat was covered with icicles from the freezing water and zero temperature. The transformation was unbelievable—from the beautiful young lady to a person that now resembled the wicked witch with chattering teeth. It was probably a coincidence, but she left town a few days later and never returned.

George Arnold was so close, that it seems strange he did not develop the idea of using a Lake of the Woods County liquor license on their part of the lake. A few years later the village of Warroad did that very same thing when they built the municipal liquor store on land that was dredged out of Lake of the Woods creating a land filled area within the city limits but in another county.

The new watering hole was called "Number Two" because that was its telephone number. There was a steady stream of traffic from Roseau County patronizing Number Two. The local teenagers made up a song, "Roseau drinks in the basement! Warroad drinks in the bar!"

Number Two was one of the most successful municipal liquor outlets in the state of Minnesota. It made so much money for Warroad that after Mayor George Bergland won the election by flipping a coin with his friend and opposing candidate Milt Fish

## Prohibition—Ma & Pa Teachout

(the popular vote was a tie), he eliminated all city taxes (except for dog tags). Milt and George decided things the way gentlemen used to: by a flip of a coin or a roll of the dice.

As the years went on, business in Number Two produced so much revenue for Warroad that every time there was a county wet or dry vote, Warroad was accused of voting dry to protect their monopoly on liquor sales in Roseau County.

# 14

## Chief Makes Chief

With little boundary patrol (if any) between the Canadian province of Manitoba and the state of Minnesota, on Lake of the Woods, we were able to fish our nets in adjoining Canadian water. There was a mile wide corridor between the two countries, a sort of no-man's water that both the Canadian and Minnesota fishermen shared.

One of our favorite sets was on the Canadian Bar that runs from the north tip of Buffalo Point to Stony Point. This bar is so shallow that the early settlers claimed, during low water, that you could drive a team of horses from Stony Point to Buffalo Point on top of the bar.

One day in early October, while lifting my nets on the Canadian bar, I noticed a boat drifting a couple of miles out from Guhl's Point (named after my grandfather). It was a nice calm day so I dropped my net to check the boat, in case somebody was in trouble. When I came within hailing distance I notice the boat was an inboard powered boat 16 to 18 feet long. She was riding low in the water with less than a foot of freeboard. When I pulled along side, it was Tommy Lightning, and his son John, Chippewa Indians that lived on the Canadian Indian reservation on Buffalo Point. The boat was loaded down with two huge moose that they had shot while hunting in the Reed River area.

My mother and Tommy were friends way-back when my Grandfather moved his family to Warroad in the late 1890's. While still a young man, Tommy nicked himself in the leg while skinning out a moose at Reed River. It became infected with blood poisoning and was amputated close to his hip. He used crutches for the rest of his life. In the summer all his hunting and trapping was done from his birchbark canoe. In the winter he used an Indian pony and sled to run his trapline.

They were on their way back home when the little one cylinder Red Wing engine refused to run because of water in the gas. John and I soon had the little "put-put" going and they continued on their way home. I watched them praying that a wind would not come up and swamp them.

Attending high school with John, we became friends and I learned about his people from the stories he told me. John was the first Indian to attend and graduate from Warroad High School. Born on Buffalo Point, John had a dual citizenship in Canada and the United States. His memory of early childhood was always being cold during the winter months. He remembered the family wigwam smoky and crowded with family members. This structure was supported by long bent poles that formed a vent in the top allowing the smoke from the fire to escape. Usually the wigwam was crowded with two or three generations.

## 120  TIME TO FISH—TIME TO DRY NETS

For hundreds of years the wigwam provided housing for the Chippewa Indians living on the shores of Lake of the Woods. This structure was covered with birchbark, hides, and fur skins and it was still in use in the early 1900's. In the summer months the Indians slept in the open.

The wigwam was easy to move from one hunting ground to another so was suited to the nomad type of living practiced by the Indians hundred of years before the white man moved in and attempted to regulate their lives. This relationship was not kind to the Indians.

The winter was the time for storytelling. John's dad, Tommy, often told stories about hunting, trapping, about how to make cedar paddles (the Indian type paddle was long with a slender blade so it could be used to pole the canoe while harvesting wild rice). John learned how to use and build the Indians' invention, the birchbark canoe; and how to use his dog to track down mink and catch them (the local mink industry was started by Indians who caught live mink and sold them to local mink ranchers); and how to use a baited set-line to catch sturgeon. The fish was dried, salted, or smoked to preserve it for winter. During the summer the sturgeons were caught with long baited set-lines and then were staked out along the beach with a cord tied around the base of their tail. Whenever one was needed for food they would wade out and pull a nice fresh sturgeon in for supper.

Diaries from Jesuit missionaries traveling with the French explorer LaVerendrye form the first records of Indian names, births, and deaths in the Lake of the Woods area. To the Chippewa, a name was not a permanent thing to be worn throughout life. Many a young warrior shed a childhood name and assumed a new one befitting his status as an adult. Tommy Lighting called my dad "Cigar Maker" because he owned a cigar factory. When I was born the Indians called me "Little Cigar Maker."

Tommy told John stories about the dead, their distant ancestors, like the warrior Auchagah who gave the explorer LaVerendrye a birchbark map in 1728. In 1732 he arrived at *Lac des Bois* (Lake of the Woods) passing through *Tecamamiouen* (Rainy Lake). If he had followed Auchagah's map he could have reached the Western Sea.

The family would talk of the spirit world, of the happy hunting ground where there was no sickness, plenty of game, where the wigwam was always warm, and everybody was happy. Believing in everlasting life, they placed artifacts and baskets of food with the bodies after they were buried. Most of the graves were covered with tiny shelters that protected the tiny bags of corn, clothing and their bow and arrow. There was no vandalism in the Indian burial grounds nor were there any homeless children, they were cared for by Indian families of the tribe.

Like all Indian babies, John was called a papoose by this family. Sometimes his mother Ethel carried the new baby around the campfire singing a song meaning "We have caught the little bird," while the rest of the tribe fired guns or made noise so that John would grow up brave.

The sign language used to communicate with different tribes was so sophisticated that it was the model for the development of the modern sign language used today.

Chippewa women never allowed a baby to cry if this could be avoided by any mode of pacification, and for this reason John was somewhat "spoiled" by his mother, Ethel. Her devotion to her children was intense, and like other Indian women, she would fight with ferocity to defend them. She would stop his crying by holding him up and dancing or the cradle board, *ahdickanaugan*, would be placed in a hammock to be rocked back and forth. The board was about 24 inches long with a curved piece of wood at one end to confine the child's feet. A birch-bark liner was formed to the same shape as the cradle board. Wearing little or no clothing, the baby was tucked in, surrounded by moss. When the moss became soiled, it was removed and discarded and new moss was added. This type of disposable diaper was prepared by rubbing and pulling the moss apart until it was soft enough for baby's skin. Indian mothers dried moss over the fire to destroy the insects.

The cradle board afforded warmth and protection. The baby's arm and legs were closely confined by pinning them tightly in cloth or deerskin. This system assured the Chippewa that their children would grow straight and vigorous. Only old men were stooped in the Indian Nation. With baby's head peeking out, the board was carried on the mother's back, held by a strap across her forehead.

The mortality rate for Indian babies was devastating. Records show one Indian mother who lost nine babies; only one of her children became an adult.

When he was five, John began to pay more attention to his father, Tommy. John's dad was built solidly, about five-foot-five inches tall. He was the same height as his wife, and just as good-looking. His face was round with a burned, dark-red complexion caused by spending all his life outdoors.

John, energetic and ambitious, knew full well there was no welcome mat for Indians outside the

## Chief Makes Chief

Buffalo Point Reservation. The only answer was to get an education. With a spotty elementary attendance, he enrolled in Warroad High School. An expert mink and muskrat trapper, he would run his trap line before school. Agile and with a slight build, he could outrun anybody in high school.

In sports competition, John excelled in basketball in which he was coached by Gus Young. As a member of the 1933 Warroad high school team, he and his teammates had the honor to represent the school in region play. Competing against class A schools like Bemidji they fought hard but were defeated, the only Warroad basketball team to ever advance to Region play.

Receiving a basketball scholarship from Carleton College, John was again coached by Gus Young, now head coach at Carleton. John continued to play college basketball until he enlisted in the Navy. He loved the Navy and spent his entire career of 30 years on fleet duty. Serving through three wars, he was awarded nearly every Navy medal including two Purple Hearts.

When he was promoted to Chief Petty Officer, the fleet newspaper carried a front page picture of John wearing his Indian headdress. The headline was, "Chief makes Chief."

Finishing his Navy career as a recruiting officer, John taught college courses on the Chippewa language and culture. The most common question asked by college students was, "Why did the Indians and white people fight each other?" His answer: "For hundreds of years the Indian people lived on the high banks of the streams because it was safe from attack and floods. When the white settlers came, they settled on low lands along the streams, safe from neither attacks or floods. The fight started

**124    TIME TO FISH—TIME TO DRY NETS**

when the white settlers tried to take away the homes of the Indians living on the high banks."

From his high school years in Warroad and college, John knew education was the bridge from the high bank to the low, from yesterday to today, for his people and all people. "If I can do it, you can do it." He taught that and believed that.

John Lightning getting his Chief's cap in the Navy. John was a 30 year Navy veteran. The Fleet newspaper carried this picture with the caption, "Chief makes Chief." John was awarded almost every Navy metal including the Purple Heart.

# 15

## Armistice Day Storm.

The Native Americans had no reason to travel the main part of the Lake of the Woods during the winter. It was nothing but a desolate sea of snow and ice, void of all life other than a fox or wolf during breeding season. Nothing out there that they needed. It made no sense to them to waste time that produced nothing in return.

The white pioneers changed all that when commercial fishing produced dollars they needed to build homes, schools, roads, and prove up their land claims. Two important industries were born: commercial fishing and logging.

Horses soon replaced the handsled allowing the nets to be set out in "the deep". In later years the windsled replaced the horse. The "Big Traverse" was no longer a fish sanctuary of deep water where they were safe.

The impact of the gasoline engine changed transportation on Lake of the Woods by doing away with the use of horses and sailboats. The first automobile to venture across the ice was a Overland

Touring car driven by Barney Arnesen from Rocky Point to Warroad. He made the twelve mile trip in less time then it would take to harness up a team of horses.

The next auto used was a Ford Model T, equipped with half-tracks on the rear wheels and skis on the front. The modified Model T did work and was used by mailmen and doctors in the rural areas but they bogged down in the slush and snow on Lake of the Woods.

Today the lake has more winter ice fishermen than any of the early fishermen could have ever imagined years ago. Sophisticated electronic fish finding equipment, excellent boats and winter track machines will continue to deplete the game fish population until the fishing pressure declines, causing discouraged anglers to go elsewhere to fish. The decreased fishing pressure will rejuvenate the lake as well as encourage water recreation other than fishing.

Working our nets for the late tullibees run I experienced and survived Minnesota's famous Armistice Day storm on November 11, 1940. Called the "Storm of the Century", fifty-nine people died in Minnesota. It was so wide-spread that duck hunters in the southern section either lost their lives or barely escaped. A half million turkeys froze to death along with other farm animals.

Lifting my gillnets along Buffalo Point that day, I needed all my training and experience as a commercial fishermen to get my boat and crew back to the safety of Warroad Harbor. Being the third generation of my family to work on Lake of the Woods, I grew up listening to my Grandpa's stories about working his nets with his sailboat, the *Grizzly*, back in the late 1800's. With our equipment nothing frightened

## Armistice Day Storm. 127

me out on Lake of the Woods, if grandpa could handle it with his sailboat I could too.

This year's tullibees spawning run was late. The water temperature was not cold enough to trigger their spawning mechanism. The run would last about two weeks on the shallow sandbars. Selvog Fish House was buying all we could catch at 10¢ per pound, a good price for us fishermen. If our catch was good we could make enough money in two weeks to grubstake us for the entire winter.

Fall fishing in November was risky business. Freeze-up over night could wipe out our nets or the wind and ice could block the harbor so we could not get out to pull them. My boat was a thirty foot gillnetter, the *Al's Craft*, with metal sheeting to stand ice breaking and a snug cabin that was heated with a wood stove. Because it was late we would have to hustle the spawning run, so I added another man to my crew that day. We called him "Lumpy" because of his muscular build. Nobody tried jerking Lumpy Huerd around because he could flatten them with one blow. The third member in our crew was Bill Growette. Bill liked to drink and raise a little hell now and then, but he was a top lake man.

On this particular day, we were towing my sixteen foot lifting boat. When we arrived at Buffalo Point it was beginning to turn cold enough to freeze ice in the bilge of my boat, a very dangerous condition because you can not pump out the water. The south wind was increasing along with ice building up on the deck and cabin window. Remembering Dad's advice, "There's a time to fish and a time to dry nets," I dropped Bill and Lumpy off at the upwind buoy.

## 128 TIME TO FISH—TIME TO DRY NETS

"Pull and pick fish at the same time," I shouted. "The bilge pump is plugged up and I am going to drift while I go below deck to repair it."

A half an hour later when I came back on deck it was starting to blow and snow. The snowflakes, big as baseballs, were driven by a howling wind that was to reach gale force of 75 mph. With no visibility, I felt a jag of fear for the safety of Bill and "Lumpy". If I did not find them, they would perish in that open boat.

Running a compass course straight into the south wind, I almost ran into them before I was able to stop. While we pulled the rest of the nets into the back of the launch, huge waves were smashing us around. We had no visibility. I set our compass course for the Warroad Harbor entrance light. Pounding into huge waves they seemed to grow higher and deeper each minute. The *Al's Craft* was not responding like it should, weighted down with ice it could barely raise its bow for the next wave.

We knew that if we were off course, or if the compass was wrong, or if my running time was off, we were in big trouble. Like magic the snow cleared for a second and there was the "blinker", the entrance light to the harbor.

Employed by the Coast Guard to maintain navigation aids on the lake, it was my job to remove all the lights and buoys before freeze- up. In the case of the harbor entrance light, the lamp was the most valuable so I decided to stop and pull it off the tower. With the lamp on board I reversed away from the structure and followed my compass course into the harbor. Lumpy and Bill used a sounding line on each side of the boat to make sure I did not drift out of the channel.

## Armistice Day Storm.

The interesting end to this story happened the next morning when I started up the engine, warmed it up, and untied the boat to take it to dry dock. When I shifted into reverse, the propeller fell off without the boat moving one inch. If that had happened when I removed the lamp, we would have lost power and never made it into the harbor. This story would never have been told.

# 16

## Northwest Angle Logging.

To some of the early Lake of the Woods pioneers, commercial fishing provided their livelihood in the summer while logging did the same thing in the winter. The early settlers were very good at working with their hands so logging and commercial fishing were natural occupations for them. Without those two industries, most of them would have moved on and "War Road", as it was called then, would not have attracted the Scandinavian residents along with a number of Germans and Frenchmen. Fishermen, farmers and loggers prospered from the bountiful resources of Lake of the Woods. Warroad soon became the main port on Lake of the Woods, home base for the expanding commercial fisheries and logging industries.

In the late 1800's and early 1900's logging was the number one industry especially when the timber could be cut along the shores of the lake. Water transportation enabled floating booms of saw logs to move to the saw mills in Spooner, across the Rainy River from Baudette. The sight of powerful steam-

## Northwest Angle Logging.

boats belching black smoke while towing log booms a quarter mile across, will never be seen on Lake of the Woods again.

The timber was skidded out on the ice during the winter where it was encircled with huge boom logs all chained together. After spring breakup the booms would be anchored, waiting for the tugs. Nearly all of the early logging was done on the Canadian side. Islands like Big Island were a logger's dream, covered with virgin pine just waiting for the axe. Sections of the island had never been touched by man before. Big Island was also a short tow to the mill in Spooner. Old pine tree stumps measuring four to five feet across can still be found on the island.

Stormy weather could break up a log boom and if that happened it would take days for crews in small boats to collect up the scattered logs. If the drifting logs were not retrieved, they became water logged, creating navigation hazards.

The early days, logging was done using hand tools and horse power. The most common timber was pine, spruce, cedar, aspen, and tamarack. Expansion of the railroads along with settlements of the western United States created such a demand that the timber industry could not supply the market.

Local saw mills like A.J. Landby's in Swift (I remember Dad buying fourteen inch wide clear pine boards for mink cages) sold lumber for $35 a thousand board feet. There was very little lumber imported at that time. Aspen was used for house sheeting while tamarack was used for bridge piling, firewood and decking.

Marvin Lumber and Cedar Company was the Warroad timber dealer, buying railroad ties and pulp wood from local loggers. In 1909, George Marvin, founder of the company, handled 30,000 cords of pulpwood. The local logging industry employed 500 men and produced $100,000 worth of timber a year. Railroad ties were hand-hewed with a broad-ax and delivered to Warroad on bob sleds where they were graded and hand-loaded on railroad cars during the winter months. The ties were not treated, so each town had a section crew replacing ties and repairing the roadbed. Just like out in the bush, the railroad section hands did all repair work by hand. A shovel and maul to drive railroad spikes were his tools while the logger used only an axe and saw. His tools improved very little until the Swede saw was smuggled into the logging camps by Swedish loggers carrying the flexible blade rolled up in their jacket pockets. This saw replaced the old crosscut that was slow and heavy. The Swede saw was a thin flexible blade that required experienced loggers to file the blade so it would not bind or kink. In the hands of a professional logger, this saw could cut off a tree with the same speed as a chain saw. The difference was, one would get tired while the other never did as long as the gasoline held out.

Then and today, logging is a dangerous occupation. To anybody who has ever worked in the bush, when the cry "timber" is heard you are scrambling to get out of the way of the falling tree. If the tree is listing or brittle it can fall out of control, kicking backwards from the stump causing injury or death to the logger.

The skidder was the most important man of any logging camp. His equipment was a team of horses and a homemade dray, that held a cord or so of 100 inch long wood. His job was to haul the wood out of the bush where the cutters piled it along side their cutting strip. Unloading it on the landing, it was

## Northwest Angle Logging.

ready for the trucks to transfer it to the railroad for shipment. The dray was made from birch or oak trees strong enough to stand the battering of stumps and rocks while hauling the wood through the bush to the landing.

All loggers were paid on a piecemeal basis: the cutters for each stick cut, the skidders so much for each cord of wood they hauled to the landing. It was not an easy nor very profitable way to make a living.

Most large camps used "strip cutting" a system where each lumberjack was assigned a strip marked by blazed trees on each side. He must stay in that strip or he was in trouble from the other lumberjacks cutting next to him. Each cutter hand-carried and piled their wood along the edge of their strips so it could be hauled by the skidders after the checkers had counted each stick in the pile.

In 1940, Moose Hilborne and I became the first commercial loggers to invest in the Stony Point area. We located our camp on Moose's old homestead where he and his brother Lloyd were camping when their brother, Rupert, drown while pulling nets in 1917. We patched up their old log cabin for our crew of lumberjacks, some local and others transient. They were called "shackers" because they did their own cooking and housekeeping.

In charge of transportation, Colin Meeker knew all there was to know about treacherous Stony Creek. He grew up there and while living with his dad, Dale Meeker, he learned not to trust the ice during the winter months. The creek is a meandering stream, crooked and unpredictable, pock-marked with underground springs that seeps up from the bottom and never freezes during the winter.

After dropping one of our trucks through the ice we made a road down the Canadian and U.S. Boundary line to the main lakeshore. Our skidder was Shell Norviak, an expert teamster that not only moved our wood but also did some cutting. By the time the spring thaw arrived Shell had our wood out on the landing waiting for Ernie Carpenter and his brother Dave to truck it across the ice to Warroad. All loading and unloading was done by hand, making it hard work every inch of the way until it was loaded into box cars for shipment to the paper mills. Our Stony Point venture was more of a learning experience than an earning one.

Enlisting in the Army Air Force after the attack on Pearl Harbor, I left the logging to my partner Moose and my brother Dorrance. They bulldozed the first connecting road to Stony Point and hauled their wood from Stony to Moose Lake in Canada, then across the border on into Warroad.

After the end of World War II, Minnesota & Ontario (M&O) paper mill from International Falls purchased the Indian owned timber stumpage on thousands of acres of virgin timber in Northwest Angle.

They began moving the first timber by truck to Longworth and Warroad for rail shipment to the International Falls paper mill in 1950. Thousands of cords of jackpine and spruce were also piled on the ice for delivery to Kenora in giant sized log booms.

It was to take M&O twenty five years to cut the Northwest Angle contract. It is estimated that over that year period, they probably harvested a half million cords of pulpwood setting a Minnesota record that will never be equaled again.

At times, M&O used over 100 lumberjacks during the winter months to complete the stumpage contract they had signed with the Red Lake Indian Council. Five independent sub-contractors each operated

## Northwest Angle Logging.

their own camp complete with cabins for the lumber jacks, cooks, scalers, skidders, and truckers. Local contractors were Norman Hohn, Clifford Comstock, Ray O'Donnell, Norman Carlson, Ernie Carpenter, and Dick Brown. M&O supervisor was Don Richards and Clarence Selvog was the company scaler. Rick Holmgren was the trucking contractor.

Mrs. Ernie Carpenter spent twenty five years with her husband Ernie, helping him operate their camp. She recalled a number of fond memories, like Bush pilot Don Hanson's airdrop of a hind quarter of frozen beef that went right through the roof of the cook shack landing on top of the cook stove. One of her most memorable stories happened to Ernie when he parked his Caterpillar in the spring only to find it had disappeared when he returned that fall to open his camp. Searching for his "cat" he found only the exhaust pipe sticking out of the muskeg! It had sunk out of sight into the muskeg during the summer months.

Another favorite story of hers was about the Shanty Man Preacher who helped make the lumberjack's life more bearable by playing the accordion while leading the camp in singing hymns every Sunday. He was a pretty good preacher, too.

The greatest pulp cutting contest in twenty years was played out at Northwest Angle when Byron Milender cut 785 sticks of pulpwood to beat Mark Cole's old record of 742 sticks. The rules were each cutter must work alone for one day. The camp average was 200 sticks per day.

When bush pilot Don Hanson circled your camp three times it meant an emergency, you were supposed to check with the M&O office and leave immediately for town.

Today Stony Point is an inhospitable, mosquito infested point full of bulrushes and marshland, and a wildlife refuge of ducks and geese. Today there are no indications that Stony Creek was once the home to a settlement of commercial fishermen and loggers.

A few tales of those days still linger on, like this story told to me by Harry Brewster when he lived there with his three brothers:

The tranquility of the settlement was shattered on a summer day when they saw a nude man straddling a log paddling furiously down the creek towards the open lake. Harry and his brother Roy started after him in Harry's new 14-foot lifting boat. They caught the man half a mile outside of Stony Creek in the open waters outside the harbor. When they tried to get hold of him he would lock his long legs around the log and roll over and over like an Eskimo in a kayak. Coming up with both arms he knocked out Harry's front tooth with one mighty blow. An enraged Harry jumped out of the boat and wrapped a rope around him. Back at Harry's cabin they used a table cloth to improvise a straight jacket before they dared load him into their boat for the trip to Warroad. The only case of a Stony Point resident that became afflicted with cabin fever.

*Top:* Northwest Angle logging by the old M&O Paper Company of International Falls. The stumpage was purchased from the Red Lake Indian Tribe. The wood was cut into 100 inch long sticks by five contractors with crews up to 100 men in each camp. Each cutter was paid for piece work: so much per stick. The picture shows strip cutting with each cutter's wood marked. This giant cut lasted thirty years.
*Bottom:* Don Richards, M&O supervisor, checking the wood piled on the ice in Northwest Angle Inlet. This wood was boomed up to Kenora in the summer months.

# 17

## Warroad Mink Ranching

Competition in the fur business was created when Charles II of England granted the Hudson's Bay Company its charter in 1670. Searching for fur pelts, the company began to penetrate into the territory acquired by the French adventurers and missionaries.

The 14,000 islands in Lake of the Woods were a great storehouse of important pelts like mink, beaver, muskrat, and fox. In the dry, cold climate, the underfur became soft and silky, covered with thick guard hair. The luxurious quality of Lake of the Woods furs became known in all the major world fur markets and fetched premium prices. Hudson's Bay Company soon dominated the world fur markets.

By the 1930's the professional trapper in the Rainy River Basin was beginning to disappear, along with the demand for long-haired fur. Women now wanted to appear thin rather than buxom. Mink coats, with their short nap and light weight, were designed to enhance a woman's figure.

## Warroad Mink Ranching

Pioneer fur farmers like George Heinen, "Shorty" Joyce, Frank Glessner and Al Johnston (my father) knew nothing about raising mink, nor did anybody else back in the 1920's. One thing they did know; the slim, carnivorous mammals' fur was soft, thick, and valuable. One thing they did not know; the mink's strange behavior patterns.

Nocturnal by nature, mink are nervous, excitable, vicious, and equally at home on the land or in the water. Leading a solitary life, they even avoid each other.

A courageous animal, smaller than a pet cat, a mink would charge anything if it was in danger, including a man. Today, the ranch-raised mink are not as vicious as that wild-caught male.

On our first commercial mink ranch, a wild-caught male flew out of his pen into the face of my brother Dorrance and locked its powerful jaws onto his cheekbone, refusing to let go. Dad and I used an iron rod to pry open the mink's mouth so we could free Dorrance.

Dad's first mink ranch was in Warroad down Lake Street. He started with five females and one male, all wild caught by local Indian trappers. Dad invented a system of cages that were connected with chutes leading from one cage to another. By the use of gates he could channel the male into the females cage for breeding. This system resulted in a high death rate for females, killed by the male after he bred her.

After Dad learned more about mink breeding cycles, this primitive system soon gave way to carrying the female to the male cage where she could be watched and removed before either the male killed her in a fight or she gave the male such a severe beating he would never go near another female. A polygamist by nature, one male could breed a couple dozen different females during the 30-day breeding cycle in March.

Using rough fish from Lake of the Woods, supplemented by North Dakota jack rabbits, the Warroad mink ranchers soon learned to feed a balanced diet that produced a kit average of four. Born in April and May with a prodigious appetite, the kits grew into mature animals which were ready for pelting in November. With high fur prices and cheap feed, Warroad was soon called the "mink capital" of Minnesota, creating year around employment for about a hundred men and double that amount during pelting season.

Financially, mink ranching was like riding a roller coaster, with nothing but highs and lows caused by the whims of fashion. When mini-skirts became fashionable, for example, skirts were going up while fur prices were going down. Once while I was attending a Hudson's Bay fur auction sale in New York City, the auctioneer stopped the sale to announce the purchase of a black mink coat by Jackie Kennedy, wife of the new president-elect John Kennedy. Like magic, the sluggish dark mink market reversed itself into a roaring bull market.

In the early 1950's, Warroad mink rancher George Schultz found a reddish-colored kit in a new born mink litter that looked different than the rest. By experimental breeding, he developed a new color strain. George later pelted out his ranch to manage the municipal liquor store. He sold the new mutation, Amber Gold, to the Heinen mink ranch.

Spanning a period of two decades and involving hundreds of mink and guidance from the best mink genetic experts in the industry, this Warroad ranch was the first in the world to produce a pink mink called Rolvalia. This pink shade is delicate and fragile like the colors of the rainbow. George Schultz's mink ranch, where the pink mutation was first noticed, was in the area of the present Warroad Town Houses.

In 1946, my brother-in-law Forest Henderson and I decided to seek fame and fortune by starting a mink ranch. After my four years in the Air Force, I think the fortune part was the most appealing. The new partnership started out with one major problem: we had neither mink nor money to buy any. In desperation we promoted a risky scheme to raise capital for our venture. We would sell breeder females to investors for $75.00 apiece with a guarantee, to the investor, of a 100% return on their investment. We would give them one mink pelt, each year for each female purchased from us. The money rolled in so fast we were scrambling around trying to buy up breeding stock to cover our sales.

Unable to breed the red-tinge color out of our standard dark mink, we began searching for a jet-black mink with thick, silky underfur covered with short, thick guard hair. We found what we wanted on a mink ranch in Utah. The mink were not large, but looked like they were coated with a black lacquer. Cross breeding the Utah mink with our own seemed to improve the color each year up through 1957 when we offered our first pelt collection in the January New York Auction sale.

Our dark pelts brought $46.50 a piece for males and $28.50 for females, topping the New York market. Nationwide publicity from the *Women's Wear Daily* (New York fashion paper) established us as one of the top mink producers in the country.

I think the most beautiful mink of all time was the Sapphire, developed by Wisconsin ranchers,

Bock & Mohr. We bought breeding stock from them and began to develop our Breath of Spring Sapphire herd. The Breath of Spring accentuated the Sapphire's delicate blue color by light blue guard hair.

Our first collection of Breath of Spring was in 1958. All five top lots (30 matched skins, enough for a jacket) topped the market at $69 each, a new record high for the entire year in New York. *Women's Wear Daily* described them as "the most gorgeous collection of Sapphire mink pelts in New York." Our record price was to stand for the entire year.

Changes in fashion plus over production caused hundreds of ranches to pelt out in the next few years. In the Warroad area only two large mink ranches were able to ride out the market. Today there is only one ranch still operating, the Heinen mink ranch.

Dad called fur farming "a skin game." He told me, "Fur farming's a hard life, but a good one. With some ambition and some drive, you can succeed. Need some intelligence, too, I guess. But not too much", he added.

*Top:* The author holding a bundle of standard dark mink pelts from his Blue Mist Fur Farm. The pelts topped the New York market.
*Bottom:* A rare Sapphire Breath O' Spring mutation mink.

***Top:*** Clayton Johnson holding a prize winning Hedlund White mink when he was ranch foreman at the my Blue Mist Fur Farm. I am grading the mink for color, quality and texture. White mink pelts from the Blue Mist Fur Farm topped the New York fur market. Note the heavy mitts Clayton is wearing to protect his hands. The mink is a ferocious animal with tremendous strength and courage.
***Bottom:*** Maggie Lightning Aas finishing fleshing mink skins. They would then be dried and prepared for shipping to the fur auctions in New York.

# 18

## Hunting and Icing Down

Freeze-up time on Lake of the Woods varies from year to year. It always happens during the month of November. By early November, cold weather will usually seal off the harbor with three to four inches of ice. The year 1948 was an exception with everything turned around. We had our cold weather in October, then November turned mild. It actually worked out just right for the commercial fishermen because the early cold weather triggered the tullibee spawning run. Temperature of the water determines when that will happen.

The tullibee is a small fish weighting about one pound that spawns in shallow water on the sandbars. When they become soft and full of spawn in November they are easy to catch on the shallow sandbars. The female run only lasts ten days before the males move in to fertilize their eggs. The eggs are golden colored (poor man's caviar), not black like the expensive and tasty sturgeon caviar.

With an average catch of 2000 pounds a day we made good money at the fishhouse price of 10¢ per pound. They are the only fish to produce caviar on Lake of the Woods, except the sturgeon. When the tullibee run was over we pulled our nets on the 14th of November. It was beautiful weather with no sign of ice or snow.

Only a few of us fishermen worked the fall run because as my Dad said, "Late fall fishing is a dangerous job, you have to know what you are doing." In bad weather and rough seas the engine can break down or your boat might roll over or fill up with water if it ices down from the freezing spray. The entire topside can become slippery when covered with ice. Snow and blizzard conditions can create limited visibility. On the Great Lakes, steel vessels crewed with professional fishermen have disappeared in fall storms.

My 30-footer, the *Al's Craft*, was ready for dry dock when my brother Dorrance and I, along with our fishing partners, Joe Oshie, and the two Hilborne boys, "Moose" and Hugh, decided to go deer hunting on Big Island in Canada. The beautiful fall weather was just too hard to resist. A few days deer hunting in Canada would allow us to unwind after a hard summer's work. The *Al's Craft* was a wood hull with iron sheathing from the waterline down. She could break up to two or three inches of ice, so we were not worried about ice, even though it was late.

While we were loading up the *Al's Craft* with plenty of food, fuel, and warm clothing, the Booth Fishery's freighter, the *Bert Steele* under the command of Captain Lawrence Saurdiff, was doing the same thing. George Boucha was the guide for the hunting party on board. It numbered fourteen local deer hunters. Their destination was Big Island, only three miles north of where we would camp on Knights Island.

## Hunting and Icing Down

It was a 35 mile trip across open water (The Big Traverse) to the best deer hunting on Lake of the Woods, Big Island. Both of us planned to hunt the next day, and return on the 16th. With no dock or harbor, the *Bert Steele* would use George's sixteen foot lifting boat to land on the beach in Patty's Bay, just across from Bridges Island on the American side. We were towing my lifting boat so we could get ashore also.

Making camp on Knight's Island, we did not see the *Bert Steele's* party, in fact we hadn't known their plans included deer hunting, the same as us. We anchored in the "gap", a no man's land, that is still under dispute between Canada and the United States. Sheltered by Big Island on the east and Knight's Island on the west it offers good anchorage. Less than a mile from Knight's Island is Canada's Hand Organ Point, connected to Big Island by a narrow sand bar. Hand Organ Point is one of the most beautiful scenic spots on Lake of the Woods.

We would camp in my cabin on Knight's Island and use the lifting boat to shuttle back and forth to Big Island. It was only one mile from the area we would hunt in. Our hunting ground was on a three mile rock ridge, close to the lakeshore, then south, to the Inland Lake and Basil Point.

The *Bert Steele's* party anchored near Bridges Island to hunt Patty's Bay and on up to Sugar Point. George posted all fourteen hunters along a strip of land that connected Sugar Point and Big Island. Years later George told me about that day's hunting, "With everybody posted, Lawrence and I used the lifting boat to circle back towards American waters. We pulled the lifting boat up on the sandbar right across from Bridges Island so we could follow the rock ridge down the center of Sugar Point. With a short drive to our posted hunters, we finished the drive in less than an hour. Listening to our gang firing we knew they had good hunting, but never in our wildest imagination did we think they would shoot sixteen deer in less than an hour."

With the deer loaded on the *Bert Steele*, Captain Saurdiff set sail for the Little Traverse. It was a beautiful hour run through islands that are still as virgin as they had been for hundreds of years. Arriving at the Canadian custom's office on Center Island, they checked the deer in. From there they proceeded down Sturgeon Channel to the Bonnie Bray resort on Oak Island. It was an excellent harbor to stay in overnight. They would leave for Warroad in the morning.

Our hunting party did not enjoy the success of George's group. Still hunting in thick brush we could hear deer but could not see the target as they crashed through the brush. Meeting Dorrance, "Moose", and Joe, they had the same luck: no deer. The weather was changing with black clouds forming in the north. It was calm but turning colder. No sign of snow. Collecting up on the beach we built a bonfire while waiting for Hugh to show up. The four of us finished our lunch with no worries about the weather. We did feel disappointed because it looked like we would return empty handed to Warroad the next day.

It was after dark when Hugh showed up and asked, "Did any of you get anything?" We assured him we had not. He continued, "I did not hear any shooting, so I assumed you were empty handed. Just before dark, I climbed up a tree hoping you boys would scare something my way." Patting the old antique buffalo rifle he was hunting with he said, "I missed the first two with this old .44 caliber Colt, but hit the next five by aiming two feet high over their backs. Not much range in these old shells, but they have tremendous impact."

The old Colt rifle was one I had borrowed from my Uncle Sid for the trip. Before we left to go hunting that morning, Hugh had said, "I have never in my life seen a lever action like this. You use my rifle, I just have to hunt with this one." He didn't even change his mind when I handed him the old box of .44 caliber bullets that were so old they had turned green from age.

Hugh told us, "We're all filled up now, so all we have to do is go and find them before the wolves do."

"But Hugh, it is pitch black out there in the bush. How are we going to find those deer without even a flashlight?"

"Just follow me, we have a couple of miles to go." He disappeared into the dark with the four of us stumbling along behind him.

It was so dark I was completely lost and hurried along to make sure I did not lose Hugh. He would stop and look for landmarks like a windfall, a big rock, or a huge tree with the top missing. Only a professional woodsman and hunter could find those deer in the dark. By midnight, we had all five deer loaded in our boat and were back to our cabin on Knight's Island.

That night the freeze-up storm moved in with a vengeance. The howling wind woke me up about 4:00 in the morning. It was snowing and blowing so hard visibility was less than half-a-mile. Checking the *Al's Craft* with my flashlight, I was relieved to see she was riding out the storm.

After breakfast we explored our options: stay at Knight's Island and freeze in, follow the Little

**150   TIME TO FISH—TIME TO DRY NETS**

Traverse to Oak Island, or try the 35-mile crossing to Warroad. We decided to try to make it back home.

Loading the lifting boat on the back deck, we started for Driftwood Point. That 12-mile run would be the most difficult pounding into a head on gale. The *Al's Craft* pounded so hard I could feel the keel flexing under my feet. Hoping the big Chrysler marine engine continued to purr along, we made our way to Driftwood.

Changing course there, we should be able to follow along Sandy Beach to Stony Point shielded from the north wind. It did not work that way. The sea was following along the beach and the huge waves made us feel like we were out in the Atlantic Ocean. Using hot water hoses from the engine, we were able to keep the windshield free of ice but the topside of the hull was coated with thick ice.

Halfway between Driftwood Point and the Stony Point reef the *Al's Craft* became unstable. Wallowing in the wave troughs we were unaware that ice was building up below the waterline on the starboard side. It was so cold that every time she rolled the exposed hull accumulated another layer of ice. None of us had experienced anything like that before. Dorrance and Hugh hung over the side and chopped the ice loose with axes whenever we rolled up on a wave.

With the worst behind us, we were close to Buffalo Point when the snow cleared just enough for us to see what looked like a "ghost ship". It was the *Bert Steele*, covered with ice and towing George's swamped lifting boat behind. Even when they disappeared in the snow, it was a comfort to know somebody else was out there.

It was dark when we tied up at Selvog Fishery dock. The running lights were covered with a foot of ice. Chopping the deer out of the ice and snow that had frozen on the rear deck, we hung them up in Selvog's Fishery to thaw out.

Leaving the fishery, my brother and I looked at the deer hanging there, "Well, Gar, we made it," I said to Dorrance using his nickname. "I wish those deer were all alive back on Big Island where they belong."

"Ya, Bo," Dorrance replied, "I wish they were too."

The *Al's Craft* the morning after the "The Hunt" in 1947 on Big Island. Late in November, it was one of the most memorable trips across Lake of the Woods I was ever to make. Battling zero temperatures and 40 mph north winds, we fought to stay afloat from daylight to dark trying to get back home to Warroad. "Long" Franson is on the boat.

# 19

## Windsledding and Two Gun

Commercial fishing under the ice was never as efficient or profitable as the summer netting operations. A few of the successful winter fishermen were my brother Dorrance, Oscar Johnson, Harry Brewster, Roy Brewster, Billy Ringling, and Fred Ringling from Warroad. The Brewster and Ringling families were pioneers in the settlement of Stony Point as a commercial fishing center. In the Long Point area, the Hoover and Neumiller families all operated both winter and summer fisheries, catching tons of tullibees for the smoked fish trade. The tullibees were the most plentiful and profitable winter-caught fish because of the volume.

The best winter fishing was during the most severe winters. The pressure ridges contracted and expanded violently during extremely cold weather, creating noise and vibrations that affect the sensitive mechanism that guides the fish under water. Experts say that the noise of a car on the ice, or a

## Windsledding and Two Gun

boat passing over the fishing area will have the same effect on the fish that a thunder storm has on us.

In the winter, the men wore layers of wool clothes, felt lined boots and homeknit wool mittens. Even when wet, the wool mittens kept their hands warm while picking the fish from the nets. Tough, strong and ambitious, these men were all professional commercial fishermen. No matter what weather conditions, in either the summer or winter, they traveled the big lake.

Basic equipment needed to operate gillnets under the ice are transportation, a heavy ice chisel, scoop shovel, burlap bags for the fish, a gillnet hook, a jigger board, and a running board. It was not as difficult to place a running line (used to pull the net under the ice) as it seems. In shallow ice a simple running board consisted of four inch wide boards nailed together to create a single strip 50 feet long. Its operation required a number of holes to be cut in the ice, each hole 50 feet apart.

The ice chisel was used as a pry to propel the board from one hole to another. Thin clear ice was necessary so the board could be seen through it. The jigger was a mechanical device six feet long and ten inches wide. Made out of a plank with sharp steel runners on each corner to guide it in a straight line, it was activated by the operator pulling on a line that was secured to a heavy iron lever that moved the jigger ahead five to ten feet each time the lever was pulled. It was used late in the season when the ice was so thick a running board could not be used.

On Lake of the Woods the windsled was developed and became the most successful mode of transportation for winter fishing. Like today, the entire lake became accessible winter or summer.

The windsled was an out-growth of the airplane, using the same principle of propulsion. It was actually an airplane without wings. If the propeller was in the front, it was called a "puller"; if the prop was in the back, it was called a "pusher." The running gear was four steam-bent oak runners with Model T Ford springs attached to each runner. The constant wind rolling the snow creates snow drifts hard enough to walk on, so riding in a windsled was like driving your car over a plowed field.

Our family's first windsled was a primitive home-built machine, like the first windsled built by Bill Radar to haul mail from Warroad to the Northwest Angle. Using a simple wood frame with no springs, we spent more time pushing the sled than riding on it. Elementary and crude, it was a simple and uncomplicated design built by my brother Dorrance in 1930. Powered with a 40 horsepower marine engine (we pulled it out of our boat), it was obvious that the builders lacked one necessary essential: money.

Even though our windsled was not a thing of beauty, its homemade wood propeller was a beauty. Five feet long, it was homemade by laminating five, straight-grained boards together. Dorrance used his engineering skill to calculate the diameter and pitch, then shaped and balanced the prop by hand.

The steering gear was a simple wooden bunk that pivoted on a steel pin through the middle of it. Located at the rear end of the sled, it would make a 360° turn "on a dime", controlled by pulleys and cables attached to a drum on the steering wheel.

Snow on the lake is different each day, depending on the temperature. Sometimes it would be good sledding; other times it would stick to the runners so hard we were unable to move.

## Windsledding and Two Gun    155

One day it was warm enough for good sledding and we decided to go wolf hunting with our new sled. The $15 bounty on each wolf was more money than some men earned in a month, so bounty hunting was not a sport—it was a business. The bounty from just one wolf would pay for our windsled. We spotted a brush wolf feeding on fish left around gillnet lifting holes used by the ice fishermen.

Using full throttle we began the chase. The wolf ran a zig-sag course for shore and safety in the timber. Following close behind him Dorrance would get close enough for me to shoot when the wolf would double back. Trying to turn fast enough to catch him, Dorrance had the sled spinning on two runners. I was hanging on for dear life trying to keep from being tossed off to the wolves, so to speak. It was a wild chase as we raced across the ice, neck-and-neck until the wolf stopped to rest. Jumping off the sled before it came to a stop, both the wolf and I were mesmerized as we stared at each other only a few feet apart. Cold and shaking I aimed and fired the old .22 caliber rifle, missing him. He stood there for a moment staring back at me, finally turning and trotting away into the timberline at Elm Point. Even though the bounty of $15 was a significant amount of money, I was glad the wolf escaped.

Recognizing that we needed a better machine, Dorrance and I drove down to the Duluth Airport where we bought a five cylinder 125 horsepower Kiner from a crashed airplane. Air-cooled, the Kiner was a good one. We were impressed by the Duluth Airport, with its modern runways and neat buildings, it was just the beginning of modern air travel.

Using a Model T Ford frame, Dorrance designed and built one of the most successful windsleds ever used on Lake of the Woods. Using the frame and suspension gear he built a fabric covered cabin heated with a tiny wood stove. On smooth ice its speed was unlimited, on rough drifts the spring suspension made it tolerable to ride in.

Another successful windsled belonged to commercial fisherman Duane Brewster. Our nick-name for him was "Two Gun" because he usually wore a gun belt with matching pearl-handled pistols. His sled was built from an old World War I airplane powered by a V8 Liberty liquid-cooled engine. In the 1950's, Two Gun decided to fish burbot under the ice using hoop nets. The burbot, used for mink feed, was saleable at four cents per pound. Setting his nets at Stony Point, he stayed there for freeze up.

It was in December before the weather was cold enough to cap the main lake with ice. With cabin fever getting the best of him he decided to fire up his windsled for a run to Warroad. There appeared to be no open water in sight. It was a 20-mile run over glare ice, with his course carrying him along the outside of the Canadian Bar to Buffalo Point, then on into Warroad. The powerful Liberty V8 pulled him along at speeds exceeding 80 mph, the runners of his sled were almost air-borne. The 30 mph north wind would record a wind-chill of over 80 degrees below zero that day, probably even colder out on the open lake.

Close to Buffalo Point, suddenly there was no sound of the runners slapping on hard ice, instead there was silence except for the swish of the propeller. Two Gun was on the wildest ride of his life over open water! Working like water-skis, the sled runners carried him along until the sled nose dived into the water and began to sink. During freeze-up water movement can create treacherous

### Windsledding and Two Gun

leads of open water. He was halfway across this one when he began swimming for his life. Reaching solid ice though, he was wasn't able to climb out on the slippery ice—until he thought to let his wool mitten freeze solid to the top of ice. If the weather won't have been as cold as it was, his mitten wouldn't have froze to the ice. Only with that froze down mitten was he able to pull himself out of the water. He lay down resting, but when he regained his strength, another danger confronted him—his frozen clothes worked like a sheet of armor and he was barely able to move his arms or legs. Crawling to his hands and knees he was able to bang his legs against the ice allowing him to stand up. Two miles away from Buffalo Point, it looked like a hopeless chance to ever reach safety.

Two Gun began dog-trotting towards Buffalo afraid to stop and rest because if he did he would never be able to move his legs again. Unable to loosen his arms he ran on with both of them outstretched looking like an aberration of a scare-crow. He suffered an occasional lapse of memory but he never lost sight of land.

Reaching shore he followed Tommy Lightning's trap line to his hunting shack where he found dry kindling, birchbark, and matches all ready for a fire. With a warm cabin he stayed there that night and dried out his clothes. The next morning he walked the eight miles to Warroad.

Two Gun's windsled is still out there on the bottom of Lake of the Woods. It was never salvaged.

*Top*: Winter burbot fishing at Stony Point. "Two Gun" Brewster on the left and I am on the right. I bought his entire catch for 4¢ per pound to feed my mink on the Blue Mist Fur Farm.

*Bottom*: Harry Brewster's windsled parked in front of his house down Lake Street. It was a good sled powered with a V8 Liberty OX, World War I vintage. He fished gillnets under the ice with it.

*Top:* "Two Gun" Brewster's windsled. It was lost when it broke through the ice on the way to Warroad from Stony Point. The airplane is a pusher belonging to bush pilot, Chet Brown. Chet used this airplane to hunt wolves for their bounty. Hugh Hilborne rode shotgun for him. Taken in the 1950's.

*Bottom:* Brother Dorrance's windsled. He designed and built this sled by himself. To power it we drove to Duluth and bought a five cylinder Velie that was for sale in the airport. Dorrance, a university trained engineer, carved the propeller out of laminated boards. Less prop pitch was used on windsled propellers than on airplanes. The sled was used for fishing under the ice. Photo, Margaret Marvin.

## 20

## Blue Water

Captain Lawrence Saurdiff, master of the Booth Fishery's *Scout* called the early fall storms "equinox storms." Equinox indicates seasonal change. In the case of Lake of the Woods, the storms always happened in October, and were always vicious storms from the North. When this cold front moved in, it created black clouds that rolled along on top of the waves creating limited visibility. Because it was the end of our summer season there was something ominous about these storms especially when you happened to get caught out on the lake in one.

On October, 1949, I was operating my gillnet outfit from Knight's Island, 35 miles from Warroad. It was my turn to go to town with our catch of fresh fish. My partner Hugh Hilborne and I carefully loaded the cargo bay with 35 boxes of fish. Each box held 50 pounds of fish covered with ice on the top and bottom. The wooden boxes cost us $1 apiece so we were careful to not smash any of them.

## Blue Water

Both World War II veterans, Hugh and I appreciated the freedom of the lake along with the chance to make good money. Our camp was only 2000 feet from uninhabited Big Island, a beautiful island with miles of sand beaches. Big Island is in Canada and is part of the Indian Reservation.

Fishing was good. The wind and cold water were moving the fish along the Big Island shoreline toward the "gap", a shallow bar midway between the U.S. and Canada. There was only room to fish two strings of gillnets across this bar. We would start the first 1000 foot string at Knight's Island. The second string ended up in no-man's land, more likely in Canada than in the U.S. We were netting two to four hundred pounds of walleye pike a day plus boxes full of perch, saugers, northern, and rough fish.

The north wind was brisk and picking up, but my course to Warroad would be with a quartering sea and my boat, the *Al's Craft*, was full beamed, a dandy downwind boat. Today's run to Warroad would take me two and a half to three hours.

The next day the lake looked formidable enough for me to have second thoughts about returning to Knight's, especially bucking a head-on sea. Yesterday's storm was now past; a "hard blow", it had reached gale force during the night, but it still made Lake of the Woods look wild and untamed with ominous black clouds rolling and swirling on top of the whitecaps.

With the help of the fishery crew I loaded up with ice and fishboxes the next morning. With the *Al's Craft* loaded, I was ready to leave hoping to arrive back at Knight's with ice and groceries for Hugh.

While loading, my boat was restlessly tugging away at her mooring lines. Probably trying to tell me, "Don't go, stay at home, forget about it, Hugh would be all right."

My premonition of disaster disappeared while I secured the cargo and tucked the heavy canvas tarp around the ice. I was ready to go. The crew untied the stern and bow lines and shouted "Good luck," as I backed away from the dock.

40 mph winds slammed into me as soon as I left the shelter of the harbor. Sheets of spray covered the deck and cabin. Setting course for Buffalo Point I pulled into the lee on the south side in a little over an hour. The first eight miles of my journey was behind me. I visually inspected my boat and cargo. Finding everything shipshape, I stood outside the cabin facing the wind, while cupping my hands to light a cigarette. In tough weather a cigarette always tasted so good.

While I was smoking, a tiny voice said, "Turn around and go back home. Hugh is all right, you do not need to go." Shaking my head I thought, "I am losing my nerve. I have made this trip many times in tough weather."

Climbing back into the cabin I pulled out around Buffalo Point into the full fury of the storm. Setting the throttle at slow speed ahead, it was slow and tedious going to Sandy Beach only to find little relief from the wind. The waves followed along the Beach, piling up in the shallow water. It looked like a winter scene from the Atlantic Ocean.

Following along Sandy Beach towards Driftwood Point was slow and difficult; everything was wet inside the cabin. After about an hour's run I changed course leaving the Beach behind me. I would now cut across the Big Traverse to Garden Island, enjoying the advantage of a quartering sea. It was the easy leg of my journey, and with the stern wind it should be the most comfortable. I was beginning to enjoy the twelve mile run across the open water to Knight's Island.

Three miles out the *Al's Craft* felt heavy as she sheared to the left while sailing down a big wave. I knew something was wrong before I even checked the bilge. It was covered with a foot of blue water, straight out of the lake.

All alone I had no chance to jettison the cargo and try to find out what was wrong. Perhaps the keel had split open or I had hit something and cracked a plank. Whatever it was I was in trouble!

Looking at my life jacket, I rejected it at once. "It is too cold, too rough, too far from shore. I cannot survive in the water."

It was a long shot but maybe the Booth Fishery freighter, the *Bert Steele*, was nearby as I was right on its course from Oak Island to Warroad. Outside the cabin I prayed to see her within hailing distance. There was nothing—only the wind, clouds, and rain. Not even a seagull was in sight.

Remembering the emergency bailer system I had installed a couple of years before, I ran to the stern to check it out. It had never been used before and was located under the floor boards. I managed to pry open the access panel only to find the two-inch cap was rusted on the pipe. I could not unscrew it. It was a very efficient system using two inch pipe connected to a hose located just in front of the propeller blades. When the screw was turning at high rpm's, the propeller created a volume water pump.

Running back into the cabin I found a butcher knife used to filet fish. Using the knife I was able to hack off the connecting rubber hose and could feel the suction as it began moving water. I needed full rpm's to move the volume of water needed to keep us floating. If I used full power and steered from the cabin I had no control over the bailer. It could plug up with trash from the bilge; should that happen my journey was over.

Hustling back into the cabin I moved the throttle to full speed ahead and felt a surge of power as the big Chrysler marine engine responded with a roar. With full power on, the bow raised up causing the bilge water to rush to the stern. Deciding to steer from the quadrant in the stern, I would screen the bailer with my fingers on my left hand to make sure it did not plug up. My right arm was long enough to reach under the stern to manually operate the boat's rudder.

With my head below the gunwales I would have to steer by watching the wave tops and my sensitive feel to the direction my boat was going. That is why I decided to continue my downwind course to Knight's Island. It was the only way I could control its direction. On my hands and knees I was already deep in water but noticed the bailer was holding its own. We were pumping out as much as was coming in.

The rest of the trip was a wild ride down the big waves with a crazy man (at least I felt a little crazy) hanging on to the rudder for dear life. My goal, Knight's Island, was safety for my boat and for me.

Arriving at the island I stood up and shouted to Hugh, who was standing on our dock, "I am sinking! Follow me!" I steered towards Big Island's sand beach and ran the *Al's Craft* full speed up on the sand bar.

When Hugh and I unloaded and pulled up the floor boards we found the shaft log (a packing box that connects the engine shaft and the propeller) had pulled loose from the keel. Held down with a dozen lag screws on each side of the box, all of them except one had pulled out. If that last one had let go I would have lost all power and the *Al's Craft* would have swamped, taking me down with her.

*Top:* "Lead and floating" gillnets on Knights Island in the 1940's. The floats were tied on with seaming twine about five feet apart to hold the net up in the water. The lead line used soft leads spaced the same distance apart. Each gillnet was five hundred feet long and two nets made up a string. Each string had a buoy and anchor at each end. It was a very movable net allowing us to follow the school of fish.

*Bottom:* My helper Charley Smith drying gillnets. Charley was a good gillnetter and always used Tide to wash his nets so they would remain soft and clean. Charley and his wife, Mary, once sacrificed a living bird by setting it adrift in a tiny cage made out of reeds. It was for their fish God because our fishing was so poor.

*Top:* Tony Cherne(right) and I gillnetting on Lake of the Woods in 1935. Note the Johnson 8 h.p. outboard. Tony and I had a near fatal accident on the Warroad River when we bounced Tony's runabout off the bow of the *Resolute*. Captain Fay Young of the *Resolute* was not happy about our navigation.

*Bottom:* Towing our 16-foot lifting boat tied close to the stern so the ice would not cut it. Powered with a 8 h.p. Johnson "kicker" we carried it in the warm cab of the Al's Craft. Note ice on the boat rails.

*Top:* Bill Growette lifting gillnets out in deep water in July when the warm water schooled the tullibees into huge schools reaching miles across. At certain times they would feed on fish flies until they bloated up making them easy to catch in our four inch mesh gill nets. This day the net was floating to the top full of tullibees. A floating gillnet was very difficult to handle.
*Bottom:* Boxing gillnets at Selvog Fishery in Warroad. The gillnet reels were used to dry gillnets when they were made of cotton or linen. The net was treated and dried once a week so we pulled a gang and set a gang every day. The net had to be boxed carefully so it could be run out without tangling up.

***Top:*** Hugh Hilborne, in the stern, with me in the bow. Our sixteen foot kicker boat on the rocky shore of Knights Island. These flat bottom boat towed easy, and handled well if they were not pulled in rough waters.
***Bottom:*** My brother Dorrance H. Johnston and Moose Hilborne holding a six foot long sturgeon. They caught it in their pound net along Buffalo Point in the 1930's. This fish weighed in at 120 pounds. A slow growing fish, it only grows about one or two pounds per year. The sturgeon is probably the most prehistoric fish in Lake of the Woods.

Alberta and I after our marriage in 1941. The Japanese sneak attack on Pearl Harbor, December 7th, 1941, forever changed the world and all of us changed with it.

Alberta and I in 1947, standing on the dock at my Knights Island fish station. Our dock and Canada were separated by the 2000 ft. "gap". It was one of the best walleye fishing spots on Lake of the Woods.

# 21

## Fall Freeze-up With D.H.

After five days of below zero weather in 1951, the first week in November left the Warroad River covered with five inches of ice. It was so cold that fall that the river ice was strong enough to support a team of horses. While some of us were trying to break out of the harbor with our boats, Don Hanson, local bush pilot, was using wheels while landing his airplane on the river in front of Selvog Fishery. It was very cold.

With thousands of dollars worth of fish nets out in the lake, the commercial fishermen were encouraged by a change in the weather. The 20 mph wind had switched to the south creating the warming trend that the Warroad fishing fleet was waiting for. A thaw would allow them to break ice out of the harbor to the main body of water that was still open. There was still a good chance they could save their nets; however, they were working in a very short time frame, once the weather turned cold again, everything would be lost.

## Fall Freeze-up With D.H.

Inside Selvog's Fishery most of the fishermen and their crews were standing around the barrel stove trying to soak up some heat after spending a couple of hours in their boats thawing out water lines, shaft logs, and self-bailer systems. Johnny LaChappelle, fishhouse foreman, kept the stove red hot, using the same dried oak wood he used to smoke fish.

The fish house, operated by George and Lucille Bergland, was a small business with only half-a-dozen fishermen as customers, most of whom were visiting with George around the stove. One by one the fish-buying stations had all vanished. Selvog's was the only fish house left on the American side of Lake of the Woods.

Standing next to George Bergland was George Boucha, the only Canadian license holder operating out of Warroad. Every gillnet he owned was frozen in across the border in Canada. George, a good fisherman, had his 30-foot launch warmed up and ready to go as soon as Dorrance (D.H.), my brother, opened the harbor channel.

D.H. had the only steel tug in the fleet. Named *Little Toot* after the children's story of that name, the tug was a good ice breaker. Next to D.H. was Ralph Kling. A tough gillnetter, Ralph had moved his nets from Garden Island hoping to cash in on the fall tullibee run along with everybody else. We could sell all the tullibee we could catch to Selvog's Fishery for 10¢ a pound.

D.H. had eighteen poundnets still fishing. This type of net is supported by piling, driven into the lake's bottom. His crew was three boats with two to three men in each boat. The rest of the fleet carried two men per boat with the exception of George Boucha who worked alone.

## TIME TO FISH—TIME TO DRY NETS

There was one thing we all knew: there was always plenty room out there in the lake every fall. Some of our best fishing could be had at this time of the year. When north winds turned cold, spray from the waves would turn to ice, causing our boats to become heavy and lose their buoyancy. Snowstorms and gale force winds could come up suddenly, causing a white out, making navigation difficult. Freeze-up weather on Lake of the Woods was no place for amateur boat operators. In fact, there was no fall traffic on the lake, except us few commercial fishermen.

The weather was clear today with no noticeable ground swell from the strong wind. With no heavy swells, there was no ice movement. The deep water outside the sand bars was still open, with the difference in water and air temperature causing a frosty vapor to roll out of the water.

The shallow water back of the sand bars, north and south of the Warroad Harbor, were covered with five to six inches of ice, plenty of ice to carry a light car. D.H had managed to break out of the harbor up to the mouth of the river, but now *Little Toot* was stuck in five inches of blue ice. She would slide up on top of the ice until she stalled and rolled on her side. Four of us walked out on the ice and climbed aboard the little tug. By moving from one side to another, we were able to rock her back and forth until the ice let go underneath her. D.H. decided to have Joe Oshie, his top pondnet operator, use his boat to push on the tug. With Joe's boat pushing we continued to rock the tug back and forth. It was moving again, but at a snail's pace.

Arriving at the harbor's jetty we could see open water three-quarters of a mile ahead. Pointing towards Warroad, D.H. said, "One of us is wrong."

## Fall Freeze-up With D.H.

Fifty feet to our right, Clarence Selvog now had a boat loaded on a bobsled and waved to us as he passed us with his Model A Ford Coupe. We watched as he drove up to the edge of the ice, unloaded his lifting boat and pushed it into the lake with two men aboard. They cranked up the outboard and headed for Selvog's Sandy Beach fish station where the Selvog pound nets were still in the water.

Now able to make its own way, I climbed off of the tug onto the ice and began walking back to Selvog's and my launch. The mild weather made the ice so slippery it was hard walking. We did not worry about the strong wind as long as it was not freezing weather. Warm and sunny I was day-dreaming of catching tons of tullibees. I would make plenty of money to see me through the winter.

Behind *Little Toot* was Ralph Kling's fishing launch and then was George Boucha's. Ralph and George were both moving through the narrow channel. They were going slow speed ahead making sure the thick ice cakes did not puncture the galvanized sheeting used to protect the wood hulls from the ice. Lumpy Huerd, my helper, was waiting for me with the *Al's Craft* all warmed up and ready to go. We pulled into the channel, trailing Ralph and George by 500 feet.

The expert handling of a fishing launch working in the ice is a stirring sight and one not likely to be seen in Warroad Harbor again. With no radio communication, we tried to keep track of each other in case of breakdowns.

When George's boat stopped, I pulled mine out of gear, thinking his engine water intake probably was clogged up with ice. When he climbed out of his boat onto the ice, I joined him to see what was wrong. Pointing ahead to Ralph Kling's boat, George said,

## 176    TIME TO FISH—TIME TO DRY NETS

"I thought I had seen it all, that nothing out here on the lake would ever surprise me, until now!" Up ahead of us, Ralph's boat was beached, lying there on top of the ice. Unable to believe our eyes, we became speechless when Ralph came sailing across the icy deck, on the seat of his pants, hitting the river ice in a heap.

The south shore ice, back of the bar, had shifted, caused by the strong south wind. The ice north of the harbor had held, anchored by Springsteel Island. In a split second the entire channel D.H. had just broken open had slammed shut like a giant vise, popping Ralph's 36-foot launch up in the air and back down on the ice with the same ease that a child uses playing the game of Tiddlywinks. The boat was on course in the center of the channel, except she was high and dry. There was no warning when the ice shifted. George and I were lucky we were still inside the harbor so our boats were not affected.

We had two major problems. One was to get Ralph's boat floating and turned around so we could get it back into the harbor. The second was to get a message to D.H.'s three boats and his crew. They were working eight miles north near Buffalo Point. There was a real danger that he might not be able to get back into the harbor again. Also, if a snowstorm should move in, he might find his men, or he might not.

George and Ralph walked back into town to get more help and to bring ice chisels, saws, and ice tongs to cut a hole large enough to float Ralph's boat again. I walked back to Selvog's Fish House to find pilot Don Hanson, who was our only hope to get a message to the D.H. crew at Buffalo Point. Don and I decided to enclose a message in a water-tight jar with a colored streamer tied to it. He would fly out

## Fall Freeze-up With D.H.

and buzz the boat, then throw out the jar, and wait to make sure it was found. I wrote, "The ice shifted and the harbor is closed tight. Come back in at once."

In a little over one hour D.H. was breaking a new channel, this time from the outside in. The channel he had made only three hours before had simply vanished. The fellows working on the ice were able to float Ralph's launch and help D.H.'s crew get back safely in the harbor.

Moose Hilborne pushing cakes of ice away from the pound boat in the Warroad Harbor. The ice was 4-5" thick, enough to carry a light car. The wood boat was "ironed" off with steel to protect the hull from the ice.

*Top:* Ralph Kling's gillnet launch after it was popped out onto the ice after the ice closed the channel shut. This boat was a typical gillnet launch. It was about 36 feet long. It carried the ice and fish, gave protection to the fishermen, and a small open lifting boat was towed to work the gillnets. *Bottom:* The toughest lake men ever to work the fall run. L to R, Bomber Dumais, Fred Moyer, John Nuemiller, Art LaChappelle, Moose Hilborn, Lew Moyer, and brother Dorrance.

*Top:* Pound net at Elm Point. This is the outside net of a double header that was cut down by shifting ice in 1954 after an early freeze-up moved the ice along the shore, cutting the nets down like a hay mower. Stakes and all were destroyed. That fall, three of us almost lost our lives while trying to salvage the net webbing. The salvage was not successful, and thousands of dollars worth of fishing gear was lost.
*Bottom*: The same net after the ice floe cut it down. Note even the pilings were cut off, and only a handful are left showing. Moving ice works just like a chain saw, everything is cut off. The small boat in the background is Bob Wenzel lifting gillnets.

*Top:* Dave Johnston and Scott Vickaryous holding a pelican that was trapped in the net. They released the huge bird and it flew away, 1970's.
*Bottom*: Unloading fish at the Selvog fishery. D.H. Johnston and Moose Hilborne facing the camera in 1947. Photos, Margaret Marvin.

***Top:*** D.H. Johnston's steel tug, *Agnes J*. This 40-footer's hull was 1/4 inch thick steel plate for breaking ice. The reels on the deck were used to pull pound nets. This sea-going tug was the last boat Dorrance was to own.
***Bottom:*** Bob Johnson(left) and Dan Marvin(right) in 1979. Note the wood fish boxes iced down with fish. Dan is holding a Northern Pike. Photos, Margaret Marvin.

D.H. Johnston's steel barge and pile driver used to set and pull pound net stakes. The tamarack piling were up to 40 feet long with a four inch top. Top picture is from the 1970's. Bottom picture is from May, 1950. Both picture are at the Selvog's Fishery. Note Cal's Cabins in the background.

# 22

## Pulling Nets

After the early November freeze-up in 1951, strong south winds continued and thawing temperatures began to loosen up the ice along the shore line. Behind the breakwater every river and harbor was still covered with thick ice but it was beginning to shift, moved by the strong wind.

The ice is never as strong in areas covered with water weeds and bulrushes. This year the early zero-degree weather froze them right into the ice. When this happens the plants embedded in the ice will weaken it because their stems work like a wick carrying warm water from the bottom through the ice to the surface. The perforated ice cracks and breaks off along the lines where the water plants are most abundant. The wind and warm weather breaks up this type of ice in ragged circular pieces, usually 10 to 20 feet across. Once the ice mass begins to move there is no way to stop it until tons of ice are piled up in huge ice mounds along the shore. We called this type of ice floe "lily pads."

## TIME TO FISH—TIME TO DRY NETS

A wind direction change to the northwest created good working conditions in the Elm Bay section. It was calm there but we did not know the westerly wind and warm weather was moving tons of ice out of the Elm Creek Bay into the open lake where it followed along the shore past Elm Point and on along the sand dunes to Buffalo Point.

The first commercial gear that the ice took out was my brother Dorrance's (D.H.) nets. The DNR only allowed poundnet fishermen to set their nets in assigned locations. D.H.'s fishing grounds began north of Springsteel Island on up past Elm point then along the south side of Buffalo Point.

Heavy tarred twine is used for the live entrapment gear used by D.H. and other pound netters. The nets are attached to piling so when the piling is destroyed by wind or ice the netting sinks to the bottom. The tarred mesh in the pot or crib must be two and one-half inches stretched measure. This type of net catches fish alive. The mesh must be small to stop them from gilling their heads as they try to escape. The length of the lead is limited to 50 rods. D.H. still had all 18 of his pound nets in when the freeze-up hit that year.

Like a pre-historic monster, the ice flow devoured everything in its path including D.H.'s pondnets. Watching from the deck of D.H.'s steel tug, Moose Hilborne, Joe Oshie, D.H., and myself were mesmerized as we watched the nets disappear one at a time as the ice floes moved over them. The net stakes snapped like toothpicks, dropping the tarred twine to the bottom of the lake.

The next day was dull and sunless, a gloomy day with the wind still blowing from the west. The four of us huddled around the fishhouse barrel stove wondering what to do. One option was to dry dock the boats and turn our backs on the lake. The other option was to give it one more try to see if we could salvage any of the nets. All experienced lakemen, the choice was easy: we would not give up until we tried it one more time.

D.H. said, "There might be a chance we can use a drag to hook on to some of the twine now on the bottom. If we take the open pond boat along, we can pull the twine into it until it is loaded, then transfer the load to the tug." He paused, "It will be tricky working in the ice but I will keep the tug outside the ice floe, keeping my eye on you with the binoculars."

Joe Oshie, D.H.'s top lakeman, was the pound boat operator, while Moose and I made up the rest of the crew. D.H. used the tug, with its steel propeller, to tow us through the heavy ice jam at the mouth of the harbor. The pond boat's bronze propeller could bend if it hit heavy ice, so we had to be very careful. It was imperative that we be able to maneuver in order to pull any of the twine.

The entire lake was hazy and bleak looking. We could barely make out Elm Point, although it was only a thirty-minute run from Warroad Harbor. The 25-foot pond boat was open, had a wood hull, and a tiny cabin and engine compartment located midship. Dad and Dorrance had built her during the winter months using cyprus planking over the steam-bent white oak frame. Designed by Dorrance, they used steel sheathing to cover the wood planking on the bottom so she could be used in the fall to break ice.

When lifting pound nets, the pot (holding crib), would be loosened up on all four corners by releasing ropes that passed through the "trip chain" on each corner stake. The loose webbing was pulled

## 186 TIME TO FISH—TIME TO DRY NETS

into the boat until a pocket was formed holding the live fish. The fish were then removed by using a dip net and were put into a sorting box where undersized fish were separated and returned to the lake. Crowducks (cormorants), pelicans, and loons were always present around all live gear. It was a good place for them to feed on the entrapped fish. They would land inside the cribs, dive down, and feed on fish until they were unable to fly back out of the enclosure. This late in the year all the ducks and loons were gone; the only bird left on the lake would be a few pelicans and crowducks waiting for fish.

We were experienced enough to know our job would be much more difficult than we had even imagined. Working in heavy ice is dangerous, especially when we would be loading the boat down with heavy tarred nets. Anything can happen and it did.

Before taking off in the pond boat we got orders from D.H., "Be careful and wave an oiler jacket if you get in trouble and need help." Joe pulled down to slow ahead and we began picking our way through the huge lily pads of ice, many of which were ten feet across and would support a couple of men. Dropping our net drag over the stern, Moose and I waited for the drag to hook on to a net.

When the dragline tightened up I shouted to Joe, "Out of gear, we got one." Looking out to where D.H. was waiting in the tug, I noticed that the tug seemed a long ways away. There was nothing but ice between us.

The three of us worked the dragline around to the side of the boat where we could pull on it. Slow but sure, we began to raise the net off the bottom. As soon as we pulled the twine out of water, it would freeze, making it difficult to pile up in the boat. It

## Pulling Nets 187

was so heavy and slippery that even a powerful man, like Moose was having trouble.

Concentrating on pulling in twine, we paid no attention to anything else, until I experienced a feeling that everything was not as it should be. Our boat seemed to be racing along through the ice but that could not be because we were held in one place by the net we were pulling. Alarmed, I looked toward the timberline and lined up two tall pine trees. We were not moving, it only seemed like we were because the entire ice pack had begun to move.

With the pond net only half pulled into the boat, it anchored us in one spot. Our position now became untenable. The ice could crush our boat or at the very least punch a hole in it.

I shouted to Moose and Joe, "The ice is shifting, we have to get out of here! We must throw the net overboard so we can move along with the ice!"

As soon as we did that, the boat no longer listed from the ice pushing on it. With everything under control, we were sailing along with the ice until the starboard side began to rise up. Hearing a crunching sound, we were now snagged on net stakes that the ice had broken off at just below the waterline. Our situation was precarious. We would soon capsize unless we were able to get off the submerged stakes.

Moose was frantically waving his oiler jacket, as the port side of our boat was just above the water. We were listing like a sailboat tacking under full sail. Dorrance was heading into the ice floe to help us.

"Joe, we are going over unless we get off these stakes. Put it in gear, reverse, forward, anything to try and move us!" I shouted. By this time, we were having trouble trying to stand up on the listing deck.

Starting up the engine, Joe said, "We will take the prop and rudder right off if I put it into gear."

Frightened and excited, I cried, "Do it." Gunning the engine, he slammed the engine into forward and then reverse, we lurched backward and bounced off the stakes. With a bent propeller and a missing rudder, we had no steerage but were on an even keel moving along with the ice flow when Dorrance pulled up along side and heaved us a towline.

"That's enough for this year, we're going home," he shouted.

# 23

# Driftwood Point Accident

Lake of the Woods is a shallow lake (30 to 40 feet deep) with scattered rock formations covering hundreds of square acres of its bottom. Many of the rocks are small and bedded down in the soft murky lake bottom. Other rock formations pile up and become reefs like Arnesen's, Archie's, Boundary (12 mile), Gull Rock, Stony Point, and the Garden Island and Knights' Island shoals, to name only a few. In some sections huge boulders are a hazard to navigation. The boulders can be shifted by the ice creating navigation hazards in new locations.

Driftwood Point, a part of the mainland, is located on the northshore thirty miles northeast of Warroad. It is a treeless area that is located between the lake and the treeline. With the same soil characteristics as the Arctic tundra, it supports low-growing vegetation such as mosses and stunted shrubs making it a fascinating area that is seldom visited by tourists. Its shoreline is covered with thousands of pieces of driftwood, a paradise for beachcombers. Employed by the Coast Guard, (my job classifica-

**190 TIME TO FISH—TIME TO DRY NETS**

tion was Lamp Lighter) I was maintenance man for the Lake of the Woods' navigation aids. In my thirty-six years of service, Driftwood Point was the only location that we could not hold nor maintain a navigation aid. In that time interval we lost four towers due to ice shove.

Each year the shoreline changed. It never appeared the same. Sometimes the tower would be ten feet from the shore; other times it would be high and dry. The first lighthouse was built there by Norman Severson in the 1930's. His crew was Bill Growette, Lumpy Huerd, and myself. We mixed the cement footings by hand, no cement mixer except our shovels. It lasted a few years before the ice destroyed it. In contrast, the lighthouse on Oak Island was built at the same time and is still operational. In 1950 while I was operating the Knights Island fishery, Captain Saurdiff of the Booth Fishery's freighter *Bert Steele* called me up to report the Driftwood Point light was out. At that time Hugh Hilborne and I were running our gillnets on the Knights' Island Shoal. Hugh was staying at our Knights Island fishing station where I was to meet him the next day.

I felt we could finish up at Knights Island, then make the hour run to Driftwood and repair the light. I knew it would be a close schedule to get there before dark. The south wind was turning into a squall line caused by the replacement of a warm air current by cold air. On shore winds would make it difficult as well as tricky to navigate in the shallow water around the tower. Backing up against a sea was always hard because it is impossible to control the steerage.

Arriving at Driftwood Point, it was already getting dark. The squall had the makings of a dangerous storm with black clouds blocking out the sunlight. Breaking waves made the beach a beautiful sight. White water seems so peaceful, yet it always fascinates me because of it's two faces, beautiful but dangerous. While easing the *Al's Craft* bow up to the tower, Hugh was playing out a stern anchor line. Everything was going smooth. The stern anchor line was our insurance policy. It was the only thing keeping our boat from washing up on the Driftwood Point beach. Grasping the tower ladder, I climbed up and repaired the light.

By the time I was through it was dark, the "pitch black" kind that can only be found out on the lake where there is not a shore light in sight. I hurried into the cabin and started up the engine while shouting to Hugh, "Stand by that stern line and snub up the slack while I reverse the engine."

In order to move against the waves I increased power until we were full speed astern and began moving away from the shore. Just when I thought we were free and in deep enough water to turn around, Bang! The boat stopped dead throwing both Hugh and I to the deck. By the time we were able to scramble to our feet, our boat was awash on the beach. With the sea pounding her she could not last the night out. If we abandoned her we would lose her. It was now so dark we could not see each other. We never knew what we hit but I believe it was a huge boulder that the spring ice moved into the tower approach.

Our first job was to free our 16-foot lifting boat and get aboard it before she swamped on the beach. The only items we removed from the *Al's Craft* were the anchor and chain. Starting the outboard on the lifting boat we headed into the wind pulling the anchor chain behind us. A hundred feet out the chain tightened and we began a steady pull on the launch hoping we could swing the bow out so she would not swamp.

Against all odds we began to feel something different, we were beginning to move against the sea. Slowly the *Al's Craft* began to edge off the beach. Although we could not see her, we could feel we were in deep water. The waves were not so sharp with no breakers. We anchored her in deep water to began a hull examination.

It was a miracle we were able to pull her off the beach. How else can you explain an old Johnson outboard (8 hp) pulling a 30-foot launch off of a beach against squall winds? Atheists don't believe in miracles, but if I had one riding with me that night I think he would have converted to my point of view.

First thing we did was to examine the hull for leaks. Next we checked the propeller shaft only to find propeller damage. The screw would turn but at a low rpm. Pulling off my oilers I slipped over the stern, into the lake, so I could check out the rudder. It was a mess. I thought if I could secure a line to it perhaps we could jury-rig a lever strong enough to force the rudder to one side or the other by exerting pressure on the attached lines. It was a slow painful trip to Warroad and we arrived at daylight.

One day on dry dock and we repaired the damage to the rudder and propeller. The *Al's Craft* was good as new!

# 24

## *Big Moe* Fire

**H**er keel was laid in 1945 during the last year of World War II. Called *Big Moe,* the beamy 40-footer was custom designed and built in a Minnesota boatyard. Using all wood construction, she had a rakish bow, mahogany cabin structure, and white oak gunwales that gave her that trim, graceful look associated with custom built yachts. Designed and built to be used as a game warden patrol boat on Lake of the Woods, she did not look the part.

She had everything to make extended cruising comfortable. It slept four, the kitchen and bathroom were bright and cheerful, and there was a picture window on each side of the cabin. All cabin material was mahogany as well as the deck and cabin hand rails.

Her new berth was in a new boathouse located in uptown Baudette on the Rainy River. Lake of the Woods game warden Ed Phorte was the captain. To fly surveillance for Captain Phorte, Minnesota assigned their first seaplane along with a warden pilot to be stationed in Warroad. The Baudette game war-

## 194 TIME TO FISH—TIME TO DRY NETS

dens felt that additional law surveillance from the land, sea, and air was needed to track down and clean out the couple dozen commercial fishermen believed to be operating clandestine harvests of fish on Lake of the Woods.

Captain Phorte and his crew did not apprehend any outlaw commercial fishermen and the *Big Moe* soon became a white elephant to the DNR and was offered for sale. It was sold but continued to deteriorate under new owners. I bought the boat and hired Pete Heppner to tow it from Baudette to Warroad. She was dry docked on the Pick and Anderson dry dock facilities located on Government Island next to the Canadian National Railroad bridge.

A wooden boat takes constant maintenance to avoid damage to the wood planking and the oak framework. Every spring, while still in dry dock, the hull must be examined by using a sharp bladed knife to test the planking for center rot that cannot be detected by visual inspection. The waterline is the most vulnerable because it is exposed to both wet and dry conditions.

Local boat builder Bill Ringling found a couple of soft planks to replace, otherwise she was sound as a dollar. Using a blow torch to remove dozens of paint layers, we scraped her hull down to the original wood. Rubbing in layer after layer of linseed oil, we finished painting her with three coats of oil base marine paint.

With an eye towards increasing the boats performance, I decided to replace the Ford V8 flat heads with a matching pair of new V8's. At that time she was the only twin screw cruiser on the Minnesota side of the lake. With two independent drives, including twin rudders, she was a joy to handle. Using reverse power on one and forward on the other screw she would turn on a dime.

When we launched her one year later, she looked like a brand-new custom-built yacht, ready to cruise Lake of the Woods. If you love wooden boats, like I do, nothing will ever take their place.

In 1966 a heated battle was shaping up between Minnesota Governor Rolvaag and his challenger Harold LeVander. Morris Taylor, chairman of the Roseau County Republican Party, arranged for LaVander to literally "set afloat" his campaign by appearing as Warroad's honored guest in the August 14th Water Frolic celebration of that year.

I was asked to lead the boat parade from the Booth Fishery to the swimming beach, with candidate LeVander on board as my guest. The local Republicans had decked out the *Big Moe* with a LeVander sign, streamers, and a new bow flag. The *Big Moe* never looked so frolicsome as she did that day. The rest of the boat flotilla followed us down the Warroad River to Cal's dock near the swimming beach. When we docked there, our candidate hurried up the dock to give a speech to the hundreds of spectators that jammed the beach area.

Every parade has a crowd favorite and Warroad's Water Frolic was no exception. Patriarch of the Chippewa Indian tribe from Warroad and Buffalo Point, Chief Tommy Lightning and his wife Ethel were the crowd pleasers. Paddling their Indian canoe, the same one they used for trapping and wild ricing, they were the last of a proud race who resisted the ways of the white man. Comfortable and at home in their canoe, they paddled it straight as an arrow without making a ripple or a sound on the water.

## TIME TO FISH—TIME TO DRY NETS

Using the same art form taught to her by her mother, Ethel had made and decorated their Indian clothes with beads. The center of their canoe was covered with a priceless canopy of Ethel's needle work. In the bottom of the canoe, Ethel's papoose (doll) was bundled up and fastened on Ethel's cradle, *ahdickanaugan*. While they were harvesting wild rice, trapping or hunting, the Chippewa women always carried their children with them. In the bow of the canoe was a sign "Going to the Frolic". If there had been such a thing as a grand prize, Tommy and Ethel would have won it.

Another *Big Moe* trip, etched in my mind forever, was the fall Canadian deer hunting season of 1962 when my son, Alan, and I spent a week hunting on Canada's Big Island located thirty miles across Lake of the Woods on a northeast course from Warroad. At that time Big Island's deer population was at its peak. The island's second growth timber along with the abundant lake water supported an incredible deer population. Deer and black bear habitat was ideal and those two game species flourished. In some areas, it looked like a park where the bear had smashed down the undergrowth while they stretched and sharpened their claws on big ash trees. While our license allowed us a black bear, we had no interest in shooting any. Ontario's generous game laws allowed us bear, deer, ducks and geese.

Sailing out of Warroad Harbor early in the morning, we made the forty-mile trip to Center Island in three hours where we bought our Canadian hunting license. From there we followed Sturgeon Channel around the backside of Oak Island then due south to Massacre Island (where twenty Frenchmen were massacred by Sioux Indians in 1736) and on to Sugar Point on Big Island. It was only a couple of miles

## Big Moe Fire

from there to our destination, Hand Organ Point, located on the U.S. and Canadian boundary right across from Knight's Island.

The cove back of Hand Organ was a natural harbor. No matter what direction nor how hard the wind might blow, we would be safe and snug in the cove. It was difficult to get into because just below the surface a large, flat rock blocks the entrance; but once you are inside it is a beautiful harbor. Looking south, a dark edge of trees marks the beginning of the great northern pine forest that once covered Big Island. We found old sawed-off tree stumps that measured over 60 inches across.

In the early 1900's the pine was logged and the saw logs were chained together to form a barrier of floating logs that were called "log booms". Powerful steamboats towed them across the Big Traverse to the Four Mile Bay and then up the Rainy River to the saw mill in Spooner.

Using our canoe, we placed our duck decoys out near the entrance to the cove to catch the flight pattern from Patty's Bay. We simply left them there so when we tired of deer hunting we would paddle over and hunt ducks.

The beautiful red and gold foliage of the trees was lovely. It was early enough so the fall frost had not nipped the leaves yet. The undergrowth was so thick that still hunting was very difficult. It was a weird feeling to have game crashing through the bush when you could not see them, or for that matter, even see what it was. Looking back, it was an unbelievable experience for both Alan and me.

Our last adventure with the *Big Moe* was October 30, 1968, when my two sons, Alan (21) and Arthur (17), and I had a close brush with what could easily have been a tragedy, on my annual fall service trip *to* Northwest Angle. We were pulling navigation buoys just before freeze up, after a nice trip from Warroad in modest windy weather. The *Big Moe* was easy to handle with a stern wind.

It was late in the afternoon when we docked at Jake's Resort in Pine Creek. We were all done except for three channel markers in Pine Creek and three in Crow Creek. They were the last buoys to pull and we would be done with our routine fall work.

We hoped to get out of the Northwest Angle area before dark. The first leg of our journey home was to Penasse on American Point. From there we would change course to Flag Island then follow the Little Traverse to Driftwood Point. The rest of our trip would be 35 miles across open water on the Big Traverse. It was shaping up to be a miserable trip because we would be bucking strong winds all the way to Warroad. Rough night trips, in late fall, are never easy and we knew this one would be no exception.

Arthur was steering while Alan worked on the rear deck securing our load of anchors, chain, and buoys. With everything on the deck shipshape, the last thing he did was to adjust the towrope on our sturdy 18-foot Alumcraft lifting boat so it would tow better. A downwind tow causes trouble because the tow will ride the crest of a big sea until it catches up with the launch. When the launch gains speed and passes it there is so much slack in the towrope it can snap. Near Penasse and within sight of the Harold Peterson home, Alan finished his deck work and opened up the starboard engine compartment. At that moment the compartment burst into flames. I had just finished making hot dogs and coffee for our lunch and was watching him when he disappeared in the smoke. On the downwind side of the fire I was engulfed in smoke as I tried to contain the blaze with a fire extinguisher. In fact, the fire was so hot I could not get out of the cabin door to find Alan.

We had a roaring holocaust on board—the *Big Moe* was doomed. The only thing on board that was left to save was the three of us, provided Alan was still alive. I shouted to Arthur, "We have to get out of this cabin and up on the front deck. We will abandon ship by jumping overboard into the lake." We weren't able to reach the Alumcraft as the stern of the *Big Moe* was full of flames and wind kept the little boat out of reach.

By now the cabin was so full of smoke we were unable to see each other. Dropping to our hands and knees, I hung onto Arthur's belt as we crawled along the floor towards the bow where we could climb out on the deck through the front hatch. Climbing up on deck we were surprised and relieved to find Alan already there. When the fire started he jumped backward onto the gunwale and ran down along side the cabin to the front deck. Except for severe burns on his right arm and singed hair, he was all right.

Huddling on the front deck, we knew it was only a matter of minutes before we must give up and go overboard. One problem facing us was none of us had a life jacket because everything happened so fast we were unable to reach them.

It was a couple of miles to Penasse, a long cold swim in the rough water. Alan shouted, "We must get the Alumcraft. I'm going overboard and swim back and get it. If it gets too hot here, jump into the lake and stay together until I can pick you up with the Alumcraft." He disappeared over the side into the cold water.

He must carry out the execution of his plan quickly or he would not survive. A 100-foot swim in 3-foot waves, with one arm burned, in freezing water was risky, but there was no alternative if we were to survive.

The front deck now became untenable and it was obvious to Arthur and I that we must abandon the *Big Moe* at once. I shouted, "Let's go! You first, I'll follow!"

Just then Alan burst through the smoke with the Alumcraft. "Jump in as I run past the bow," he shouted. Arthur and I dove into the boat.

At the same time local bush pilot, Don Hanson, had seen the fire while on his way into Warroad. It was getting dark and he tried to land alongside us, but was unable to do so because of the big waves, so he flew across the bay and landed in the lee on Canadian waters. He waited there until we caught up with him in the Alumcraft. The burns on Alan's arm were serious and he needed medical attention at once. Don found room for him on board his Cessna float plane. They were in the air and on their way into Warroad almost before Arthur and I were able turn the boat around and head back towards the burning launch. It was weird to see a ball of fire out there in the middle of the channel.

Arthur and I returned to Norman Carlson's resort in Crow Creek, where Norman checked us into one of his cabins. Neither of us had any serious injuries except for singed eyebrows and hair. The next morning we found the skeleton of the *Big Moe* had drifted up on the muskeg. All the buoys were in a cluster near the burned hull. Except for needing a new paint job, they were not damaged.

The strong winds had pushed the fire through the cabin to the bow. Fortunately, the wind held the fire away from the fuel tanks located under the rear deck, otherwise they would have exploded. When we examined the tanks we found a loose drain plug that probably flooded the rear deck with gasoline that ignited when it leaked into the engine compartment.

The *Big Moe* at the Warroad Water Frolic, 1966. It carried dignitaries of the Minnesota Rebublican Party. The interior design of the *Big Moe* was superb and my family and I used it for both pleasure and lake work. Two years later it burned to the waterline while removing Coast Guard buoys in Angle Inlet. My two sons and I barely escaped from that fire.

Chief Tommy Lightning and his wife Ethel at the Warroad Water Frolic, 1966. Note the beadwork canapy and the papoose.

# 25

## Northwest Angle Closing

Five types of gear have been used by commercial fishermen on Lake of the Woods. These include pound nets, trap nets, hoop nets, gillnets, and ocean-type fish trawlers. Pound nets are attached to stakes driven into the lake bottom. The net has fence-like lead, funnel-shaped heart, and a pot where the catch is impounded. Length of the net's lead is 50 rods. The pound net is a very expensive gear that takes special equipment like barge-mounted pile drivers and special lifting boats. It is a volume gear that is used along the shoreline or on sandbars. Fifty pound nets are allowed on the lake.

Trap nets are similar to pound nets in all respects except the length of the lead is restricted to 400 feet and anchors instead of stakes are used to hold it. Each license is limited to ten nets. Grouped together, fyke and trap nets are restricted to eighty for the lake.

The law allowed 80,000 feet of gill nets and each licensee was allowed 4,000 feet each. The gillnet differs from other gear in that they are not staked but anchored which makes them mobile and of use in open water. Essentially they are a curtain of mesh hung between a float line and weighted lead line. The mesh size may not be less than 4 inches, and the net is thirty meshes or about 8 feet deep. With this net, fish try to swim through the webbing and, if they are large enough, find the openings too small. They are kept from backing out by the mesh which gets caught behind projecting scales or gill flaps. The gillnet is very selective in the size of fish that is caught, but the pound and trap nets is not size selective and takes a lot of large fish.

Trawls operate on the principle of towing a mesh bag on the end of tow lines behind a boat. The bag is held open on its forward motion through the water by two doors or boards, each acting in the matter of a kite holding the mesh bag open. This volume type gear is not selective and became very controversial in the years 1961 through 1964 when its use was discontinued on Lake of the Woods.

The gillnet was the "poor man's gear" because they were inexpensive to make and handle. Most gillnetters worked alone out of 16 to 18-foot long gillnet boats. The nets were set in thousand foot long strings with an anchor and marker buoy at the end of each string. The gillnet gear was to become the only profitable gear to survive the changing economics and politics on Lake of the Woods until 1985 when the last net was reeled in.

Commercial fishing creates more than its share of political controversy. It was a local issue for many years until the 1970's when the big city newspapers began to fan the fire. Soon as that happened the politician knew the fishing issue would generate votes for them.

On the other hand, the commercial fishermen were so independent it was impossible to organize them into an effective political force. Dad said, "The fishermen get all stirred up when anyone tries to take something from them. But when it comes to defending their industry they are tongue tied at public meetings."

Father Shanahan, the local Catholic priest, was one of the fishermen's first spokesman. He was a spellbinder and could debate commercial fishing with anybody. His best punch line was: "The total harvest of walleye pike and saugers is less than one half pound per acre." Then he would add, "Can you spare it?"

During War II, when most of the commercial fishermen were in the service, the sportsmen groups from Roseau and Baudette joined with DNR game warden Ed Phorte from Baudette to pull enough strings to close Northwest Angle to commercial fishing. George Arnold's American Point fishery, Art Gidding's Blackbird Island fishery, Bob Wenzel's Oak Island fishery, and Marvin French's Sugar Point fishery were all denied renewal of their fishing license in 1947.

The problem facing the DNR was, "What to do with the commercial fishermen when they were discharged from the service and came home to find their business gone?"

In order to appease the displaced veterans, the Minnesota DNR decided to make the rest of the commercial fishermen pay the bill. They used the time old system, "Rob Peter to pay Paul." The way it worked was: The law allows the gillnet license 4000 feet of gillnets. So the DNR reduced, by executive order, the amount of each gillnet license from 4000 feet to 3000 feet. They then gave the displaced,

Northwest Angle pound netters each 3,000 feet of gillnet to try and appease them. The result was to increase the gillnet fishery while decreasing the pound nets on the lake by eighteen nets. It was an apparent about face for the DNR because the DNR used to said they favored the use of live entrapment gear. In later years the DNR flip-flopped again and would say they advocated live entrapment gear in preference to gillnets but as there was no longer any live gear left on the lake, they then finally succeeded in their goal of eliminating all the commercial fishing.

It was a low blow to the fishermen by the DNR because it reduced their license footage by 25 percent. That meant catching less fish resulting in less income for each fishermen.

Flush with success the same sportsmen's groups then decided that the entire lake should be closed to netting. They found a friend in State Representative Curtis Olson from our District. Curtis was politically ambitious with hopes of becoming the Seventh District U.S. Representative.

It was after the Christmas holidays, 1950, before we were informed that Lake of the Woods commercial fishing legislation was on the House agenda and was scheduled for hearings before the Natural Resources Committee. Representative Curtis Olson was the author and sponsor of the proposed bill.

The city of Warroad rallied to the support of the commercial fishers. It was an important part of the Warroad economy and a town meeting was held. With the support of the town, the fishermen organized the Lake of the Woods Commercial Fishermen's Association. They elected a popular Long Point fisherman called "Fog Horn" Hoover as President.

Mr. Hoover was a tall man that was afraid of nobody. His voice would carry a block or so and he usually made his point with some choice words that made everybody stand up and take notice. A good fisherman, he and game warden Ed Phorte were in and out of court with various fishing infractions charged against him. None of the charges were ever proven but Mr. Hoover spent a fortune on legal fees. The story circulated that on her death bed Mrs. Hoover's last words were, "Damn warden Ed Phorte."

President Hoover appointed a committee of three to represent the commercial fishermen in St. Paul. The fact that I was a WW II Air Force veteran was why I was on the committee. My first year as a civilian I had plunged into debt, buying a new commercial fishing launch, and investing in a mink ranch partnership. If I lost my commercial fishing license there would be no way I could pay off my debt load.

The second member of our delegation was John Pick. John was very bright and attended college on a scholarship hoping to get admitted to medical school. With little or no money he dropped out of college and bought out Floyd Squire's gillnet outfit.

John was a good politician, with only one fault, he had an uncontrollable temper. He drove an old beat up, cranky Essex which never did start very well. The battery was always down so John would have to crank it by hand. In those days all autos had cranks so they could be hand started. One day John came to town to visit his friend, the town's leading politician Julius Anderson. Julius was active in the powerful Minnesota DFL Party and a friend of the commercial fishermen.

## TIME TO FISH—TIME TO DRY NETS

Leaving Anderson's Jewelry Store, John tried to start the old Essex, first running down the battery, then resorting to hand cranking it. John labored away on the crank, until it came loose and he banged his hand on the grill. By that time there was a half dozen locals standing on the sidewalk shouting suggestions on how to start the engine. Wrapping his bleeding hand in his handkerchief he took the crank and beat that old Essex to a pulp right there on main street. It was towed away to the junkyard the next day.

The third member of our delegation was Clarence Selvog, a pound netter from one of Warroad's most prominent families. Clarence was a "party animal" that loved people and was very suave and diplomatic. Tall and slender with fair hair, he was handsome when all dressed up in his expensive suits. They seemed to belong on him. He was a natural politician except his socializing at the bar could prove awkward especially when he would rather drink than eat.

Clarence Selvog called his Uncle Sever Selvog at his home in St. Paul asking for help. He told Sever that he, along with John Pick and myself, would represent the fishermen at the hearing. Sever assured him that he would help us and would reserve rooms in the St. Paul Hotel. At that time it was "the hotel" in St. Paul. Every politician, worth his salt, either stayed or hung around the cocktail lounge in the evening. Sever was a friend of the manager of the St. Paul Hotel and knew all the DNR people.

The way it turned out it was a good thing he knew the hotel manager because the three of us almost wound up in a St. Paul jail. We never did find out who, if anybody, set us up for a gambling bust in the hotel. We were just getting settled in when Clarence

## Northwest Angle Closing

answered a loud knock at our door. It was two husky fellows dressed in topcoats and soft brim felt hats. Showing us their badges they said, "We are St. Paul detectives from the vice squad. We understand you are running a floating crap game in your hotel room. Our orders are to take you in to our office." They were serious about the charge. Clarence asked, "Can I make a phone call to my uncle in St. Paul?" They said, "Sure, go ahead." Sever told Clarence to wait until the hotel manager could get up to our room.

The manager and the hotel security chief soon showed up. The manager talked to the police officers telling them, "For heaven's sake what are you trying to do? These are three commercial fishermen from way up north in Warroad. These boys are honest and would not steal a penny from anyone." The detectives were assured and we never saw them again.

Before be had left Warroad, owner of the Warroad Pioneer, Earl Chapin, gave us a sign for my car reading, "Press Warroad Pioneer." He told us, "Drive around to the rear of the Capitol building and you will find a small parking lot with a sign reading 'Press Only.'" Finding the parking lot we placed our Warroad Pioneer sign in the window. On one side of us was the St. Paul Dispatch and on the other side was the Minneapolis Tribune. The Warroad Pioneer had finally hit the big time.

With time running out, I almost forgot a bit of advice from Earl, "Never leave your keys in your car and when you lock it be sure all the windows are turned up."

While locking the car, I thought, "We never worry about anybody stealing our car in Warroad." The crime rate was so low in Warroad that the town constable was selected on a simple merit system, the fellow needed a job.

Constable "High Pockets" (he was six-foot-six) solved the only car theft on record in Warroad when my Dad's 1934 Chevy disappeared one afternoon when it was parked on Main Street in front of Joe Holland's beer parlor. Also enjoying a cool beer was George Heinen. While drinking his beer George received a phone call saying his wife was in labor. George, an excitable man, ran outside, jumped into my Dad's new car and roared away to the hospital. High Pockets solved this crime by ambling around the block until he found George's car, which was the same color and model. The car was unlocked with the keys in it so High Pockets told my dad, "We know George made a mistake and we know why he made it, so you take his car and use it until George gets this baby thing out of the way and brings yours back."

When the Warroad delegation entered the capitol building we found ourselves in a beautiful marble hallway that was crowded with people. All the men seemed to be wearing black suits and carrying matching brief cases. Compared with our outdoor, ruddy complexions, the men's pallor seemed unnatural as they hurried along.

We were waiting for Representative Curtis Olson outside the committee room. When he showed up for the hearing, his startled expression soon gave way to a hardy handshake with all three of us. He had that particular aura that seems to surround politicians in the atmosphere of the Capitol. Up there they can exercise the most powerful weapon there is, the vote. You have none.

The sportsmen groups were conspicuous violators of the rule every good lobbyist knows: "Depend on nobody to pass your legislation. You must guard it and fight for it right up to the last minute."

It was apparent Representative Olson was confident he had the votes in his pocket to push through legislation to eliminating commercial fishing on Lake of the Woods.

Seating ourselves in the committee room, the committee Chairman called on Representative Olson, as the author, to speak in support of his bill. Confident and self-assured he walked up to the podium and removed a prepared statement from his pocket, "Mr. Chairman and committee members. I do not wish to impose hardship on any of my constituents. They are hard-working friends of mine from Warroad. Tourism is the economic future of Warroad and Roseau County. The gillnets are catching all the trophy-size walleyes from Lake of the Woods. There's nothing left but tiny fish for the sport fishermen who have paid a license fee to fish." Representative Olson was most gracious, thanking the committee chairman and committee members. The Chairman then called on the DNR fisheries expert. His name was Chuck Burrows, former Navy Commander. Chuck was to dangle the commercial fishermen from a yard-arm for over thirty years.

The new fisheries expert was a graduate of the University of Minnesota and had worked with Dr. Smith, a renowned fish biologist. Chuck was smooth with a low key approach, that would disarm you; he was now opposed to the use of gillnets.

He rambled off technical data like, "We feel there is adequate brood stock to maintain maximum recruitment." He paused to let that profound statement sink in. He continued, "Good lake management practice is not differential to the method used to harvest fish if there is a crop that can be utilized.

Political expediency resulted in the addition of gillnets to the existing entrapment gear. I feel that was a mistake.

"However the DNR does not support elimination of all commercial fishing on Lake of the Lake of the Woods."

We battled Chuck Burrows for survival of our industry for over thirty years until he retired as Director of Game and Fish.

As the spokesman for our group, I addressed the committee without using any notes. I was emotionally involved and committee members knew my testimony was genuine. I believed it when I told them, "Unless rough fish are controlled they will compete with game fish for feed habitat. If the burbot, tullibees, suckers, perch, and saugers dominate the fish population there will be a proportionate decline in the walleye fishery. Should the lake experience excellent walleye spawning years an increase in numbers will slow down the growth rate as they compete for food and space. When that happens, more walleye pike will be caught in numbers, however, the fish may be small. Fish cannot be stock-piled like gold or silver. They are a renewable resource that live and die no matter what method of removal is used. Our commercial fishing industry helps to maintain a healthy fish balance by removing the rough fish."

I completed my presentation, "Commercial fishermen love the lake and will do nothing to destroy its fish population. We are small businessmen that make a living using our own two hands to remove fish from our nets. The sportsman uses his two hands to remove the embedded hook in the mouth of the fish. The only difference between the two of us: One does it for fun and the other does it to make a living."

With nothing more to say I sat down with John and Clarence. The committee chairman adjourned the meeting without asking for a vote.

We learned that committee meetings in St. Paul are manipulated by committee chairmen that will use any tactics to delay voting on any legislation they do not agree with. If you were from out of town the strategy was to wear you down until you ran out of money and had to go back home. In our case, that would not take long.

Why he confided in us was not clear, but Representative Olson told us that he was going to run for U.S Congressman from the Seventh District. In order to do that he was moving to Detroit Lakes to establish a broad voter base. His present job would be "up for grabs" and he ask me if I would be interested in running for it. We then knew where the conversation was going, Curtis wanted to make a deal.

I said, "You know and I know that as a commercial fisherman I would have about the same chance as a snowball in hell to be elected when you vacate your office. Why me?"

His answer, "In Roseau we want to have a liquor store. However, as long as Roseau County votes dry we cannot have one. We both know that we need wet votes from Warroad in order to sell liquor in the county. Your job would be to swing enough wet votes our way so we can exercise the legal option to sell liquor in Roseau."

He was referring to Warroad's municipal liquor store, called "Number Two." It was located on a jetty that projected into Lake of the Wood County. Therefore, as Lake of the Woods County was wet

Warroad's Number Two was legal. Roseau County's "party crowd" flocked to Number Two making so much money for Warroad that the Mayor declared a moratorium on local taxes.

This local "gold mine" was the envy of powerful county politicians, like Curtis and his friends. With so much money rolling in, Warroad always voted dry to keep the Roseau County business. My response to Curtis was, "I have no intention of selling my friends out, no thank you." My political career was a brief one.

Back in our room at the St. Paul Hotel after that first hearing, Clarence, John, and I knew we needed additional help to save commercial fishing on Lake of the Woods. John came up with a brilliant idea when he said, "Alvin, you are a veteran and member of the American Legion. They are working to make sure returning veterans receive their jobs back, it seems to me there are forces that want to destroy you, and your way of life as a commercial fisherman. Why not contact the St. Paul American Legion Service Officer to see if they will help you."

It was a good idea so we looked up the telephone number in the directory. I made the call and set up an appointment for that evening in the lobby of the hotel. I was waiting for him when he arrived. A pleasant young man, politically smart and experienced and he was a good listener.

After an hour or so he said, "I will help you. Nobody is going to push veterans out of business, especially the State of Minnesota. Arrange a meeting with Curtis Olson at the capitol, in the lobby underneath the dome. I will be there with an attorney friend of mine by the name of Matt Thorsen. He is an expert on game and fish laws and was the attorney that revised and recoded the new Minnesota Game and Fish laws."

I contacted Curtis and he agreed to meet with us the next morning at 9 a.m. before the House convened. The next morning I met with the American Legion Service Officer and was introduced to Attorney Matt Thorsen. Matt was a little on the shabby side wearing a wrinkled old suit.

When Curtis showed up he was startled to meet Matt and the Service Officer. He took me aside and asked, "Where did you make contact, with these two fellows? They are two of the most powerful lobbyists in St. Paul!"

Curtis tried to defend his legislative program but that did not faze either of my new friends. The American Legion Officer cut into his argument, "Curtis, you people are not going to drive veteran commercial fishermen out of business on Lake of the Woods. If you try, I will debate the issue in front of the House with you or anybody else."

Attorney Thorsen then pulled a copy of Curtis's proposed bill out of his pocket and said, "Now this is the way to straighten this thing out. The DNR can do this through the use of the Commissioner's Order. No need to pass new legislation. The Commissioner will not issue any new gillnet license, however the existing gillnetters, may continue to commercially fish their gill nets until their death."

Curtis kept nodding and saying, "Yes Matt, that sounds good, we will do it that way."

After Curtis left Matt said, "Boys, you can go home. This issue is now dead. You Lake of the Woods commercial fishermen now have a 'closed shop.' Nobody else can get in to compete with you."

The system worked for over thirty years until we tried to turn our licenses over to our children. We knew the only way was to change the law so we could transfer our license. That became our main goal in later battles.

One of the last gillnet license transfers was to my wife, Alberta, when I was in the Air Force. Head lake warden, Ed Phorte found a way to restrict commercial fishing by deciding that absent commercial fishermen, in the service, were no longer residents of Minnesota, so he denied approval of my 1943 license.

At the time I was on detached duty, flying in and out of the Twin Cities in a C47 troop carrier cargo plane. We were towing gliders from Minneapolis, where they were manufactured, to Bergstrom Field in Texas. While in Minneapolis I called on the Director of Game and Fish, Frank Blair. I explained that I had good management of my fishing outfit, and that we were trying to do our part to help the war effort. I asked him, "If I was no longer a Minnesota resident why was I sent absentee ballots for state and federal elections?" He sent me on to the DNR Commissioner who seemed to think it was wrong to deny me my license.

He did not want to overrule one of his game wardens so he asked me, "Do you have any ideas?" I suggested he transfer my license to my wife. He did that, so she became one of the few lady commercial fishermen in Minnesota. After the war the license was returned to me.

With our business completed in St. Paul, we packed up to go home the next morning. It was a nice day, a little on the cold side, but we were in good spirits—at least we were still in business. Clarence was not talking and he was curled up and sick on the back seat. Approaching St. Cloud I turned off the highway to find a hospital and doctor. Pulling alongside a police car I shouted, "Where is your hospital? We have a sick man in here." The Officer said, "Follow me."

I drove up to the emergency entrance where a nurse and hospital aid was waiting. Two hours later the Doctor came into the waiting room with bad news. He suggested we contact Clarence's wife and have her come down at once. Clarence had double pneumonia and the doctor explained it would take the sulfa medication a few hours to be effective. He was on the critical list. I called his wife, Dorothy, and she said she would leave for St. Cloud at once.

The next morning Clarence was off the critical list. John and I decided to stay a few days with his brother, Vernon, at Royalton, Minnesota. Vernon was a fascinating intellectual with a library lined with technical textbooks recommended by his academic friends like Dr. Richard Scammon and Sinclair Lewis at the University of Minnesota. All the books were scientific, engineering, and medical.

The Royalton complex was his dream of a communal-type community with a capitalistic system of free enterprise. To help make this dream come true he built an exact replica of Boulder Dam to supply his own power from Two Rivers. He had on-site power that no outside agency could tamper with.

Interested in airplanes, Vernon became a commercial pilot and ferried bombers during World War II. After the war he worked at aerial mapping, grinding his own lens to improve the quality of his pictures.

Divorced when his only daughter Virginia was six, he remarried Ruth Johnston, a Bloomington school teacher. They were married in Dr. Scammon's home with the doctor giving the bride away.

With business good, happily married, along with visits by Dr. Scammon and other University faculty, his Royalton experiment was a success. He loved deer hunting and would take time out to join his brothers John and Lloyd during deer season in the Warroad area.

Vernon, with an eye to for the unusual, enlisted the aid of Dr. Scammon to convert roe from carp into caviar. Although they had fun trying, it soon became apparent the sturgeon was more qualified to produce caviar than carp would ever be.

When fire destroyed the Royalton complex in 1951, his total insurance settlement was $13,500. With a used trailer and pickup truck and $6,000 left from his insurance, he decided to go prospecting for uranium in Utah.

He and Ruth drove to Grand Junction, Colorado, where the Colorado Plateau Atomic Energy Commission headquarters was located. AEC officials suggested the Hanksville, Utah, area near Henry Mountain and Muddy River, a desolate desert with no water or roads, with few animals, and 60 miles from the nearest telephone.

He would spend two weeks at a time in the desert, all alone on foot, with a 60 pound scintillometer (a souped-up Geiger counter with more range.)

In 1952, exactly one year after the disastrous fire at Royalton, he was out of money, dehydrated, and exhausted. Spending a few days with Ruth in their trailer home in Grand Junction, he decided to make one more two week prospecting trip.

He made only 20 miles in four days. It was slow checking the 1200-foot canyon walls along the

Muddy river. He would wade from one side to the other as he followed the river.

Stopping to dry his clothes, he looked up 400 feet to a ledge caused by rock outcropping. He decided to check the ledge out. The needle on his scintillometer was erratic and then moved off the scale. By the time he stopped to rest on the ledge, the needle had disappeared completely. At 50 years of age, Vernon had found Pick's Cliffside Uranium Mine. He later said, "I walked a step for every dollar I sold the mine for."

Without knowing the significance or value of such a find, Warroad first heard the news when Vernon called his brother, John, to come out to Utah and help him operate the mine.

The first year, John and eight other miners shipped uranium ore valued at $500,000. The ore contained up to 80% uranium, compared to the 10% average at that time. Owning 100%, he was to become Warroad's first "honest-to-goodness" millionaire.

In 1954 he sold the mine to Odium's Atlas Corporation for $9 million cash and a $250,000 PBY former navy seaplane. "Along with the $9 million, it was a good deal."

In 1970 Vernon Pick was to spend millions of dollars developing "Walden North," in British Columbia. In this private industrial estate, he followed Thoreau's philosophy in making it self-contained, with its own water power and supporting shops. The huge complex would fit into a James Bond movie. It followed Thoreau's philosophy that each man do his own thing to the best of his ability. But the only thing Pick's Walden North had in common with Thoreau's Pond was isolation.

Clarence Selvog at Sandy Beach in 1935 driving a team of mules. His dad, Hans, fished eighteen pond nets along the beach. The mules were used to put up ice, to haul fish, and to move nets. The Sandy Beach Fishery employed a crew of men the year around. Photo, Dorothy Selvog.

My friend, Bob Wenzel, tarring pound nets on Oak Island in 1939. Bob and his helper are packing the nets down so the tar will cover the twine. The tar was heated to a boiling point by building a fire under the vat. A bucket of cold water was always within reach in case the tar boiled over. In that situation the tar would catch fire unless the cold water was poured in it. The pound nets were tarred twice a year, spring and fall.

Vernon Pick was the world's and Warroad's first honest to goodness Uranium Millionaire. Prospecting on foot in the desert near Hanksville, Utah he found a Uranium mine. Selling the mine in 1954 for nine million dollars, he was called "The Uranium King" by the press. He said, "I walked a mile for every dollar". Photo, Lloyd Pick.

*Top:* Vernon Pick's renovated Navy PBY. He and Lloyd used to fly the PBY up to Alaska to go big game hunting. Vernon was known all over the world as the "Uranium King."

*Bottom:* Vernon Pick hunting wolves on Lake of the Woods. Both timber and brush wolves had a county bounty of $15.00 for brush and $25.00 for timber wolves. Hundreds of wolves were shot out on Lake of the Woods during the winter months by commercial and private pilots. Photos, Lloyd Pick.

# 26

# Battle Over Trawling

**M**ink ranching and commercial fishing became intertwined when a number of commercial fishermen became mink ranchers. It was a rollercoaster ride with unlimited capital supplied by the New York fur interests. Our dream ship was sailing home loaded down with money supplied by fur buyers who scrambled to find enough pelts for a market that still wanted more.

Every fish commercial fisherman caught was saleable for human consumption or for minkfeed. Mink ranches were everywhere, including four located inside the village limits. Three of them were owned by my family. Dad, brother Dorrance, and my brother-in-law Forest Henderson and I.

This "bull market" in the fur business, was created by a splurge of consumer buying by a luxury-starved public after four dreadful years of war. Finally the Great Depression of the Dirty Thirties was over and people were buying new homes, autos, and new clothes. People were traveling and the universities were jammed with returning

## Battle Over Trawling

veterans attending college under the GI Bill. The economy was on a roll that, with the exception of a few slack periods, is still surging ahead today. The world fur market flourished with the introduction of mutation mink like the Pastel, Sapphire, and Jet Blacks. A whole wheel of color allowed the designers to create beautiful fur garments that appealed to everybody's taste.

The fur industry reached an annual production of over ten million mink pelts a year before over production slowed it down. Along with this new prosperity, our ranches outgrew Warroad and we joined a half dozen other ranches located on the outskirts of Warroad. Modern mink ranch housing outdated the original outdoor cages. Modern refrigeration replaced our old salt and ice storage plants and we now had power feeders, skinning and fleshing machines.

Soon the local fishing industry could not supply the local demand for minkfeed. It was an economic bonanza to the commercial fishermen, pushing the market to new heights with every pound utilized everyday. The tullibees and burbot were the best minkfeed as they were no longer used for human food (due to politics and fashion). If you were a licensed commercial fishermen you were in an advantageous position if you owned your own mink ranch.

A commercial fishing license on Lake of the Woods was a valuable license. With a closed shop no new licensed fishermen could be granted a license, so the scramble to control the rough fish market was on.

The shortage of rough fish for minkfeed opened the door for Minnesota Director of Game and Fish, Chuck Burrows. Chuck used this new demand to increase the Lake of the Woods fishery harvest by issuing a Commissioner's Order to grant experimental gear on Minnesota lakes without regard to the wishes of the legislature or the acceptance of such gear by the citizens.

Chuck's idea was to replace the gillnet fishermen with ocean-going fish trawlers. He thought that the walleye should be reserved for sportsmen, but that rough fish were too valuable a resource to ignore. But the gillnet walleye harvest was difficult to control so he wanted the fishery to change gears.

The trawls operate on the principle of towing a mesh bag on the end of towlines behind a tug. The bag is held open on its forward motion through the water by two doors or boards, each acting in the manner of a kite to hold the trawl's bag open. Operating on the "reverse snow plow" principle, the fish were directed into the "cod end" where they were trapped. It was a non-selective, high volume gear, with each vessel able to produce up to two million pounds of fish during the summer season. The trawl still caught walleyes, but Burrows claimed that they could be returned unharmed back to the water.

The DNR Commissioner signed a trawl permit for two vessels to operate on Lake of the Woods for the years 1961 and 1962. Classified as "experimental" its operators needed no license nor did they need to comply with existing regulations. It was a "gold mine" to the owners who were big mink ranchers, but who previously had never been gillnetters. After two years of operation, Chuck Burrows, DNR Director of Game and Fish, was the promoter for the "trawler camp" using all the powerful weapons in the Department's arsenal of "dirty tricks".

## Battle Over Trawling

The licensed gillnet fishermen now had no contact with the DNR and they were on the outside looking in. Fearful of losing their livelihood the fishermen created any uneasy alliance with the sportsmen's clubs with one objective—to defeat the trawler. The sportsmen decided they would much rather have the small independents working the lake than wealthy companies using ocean going trawlers. Strange bedfellows, to say the least.

Unable to defeat a bill that would secure the trawler future, we compromised on a a bill that would let the trawler fish for two more years. It would come up for vote again in 1964. During that two year period the trawler issue heated up and we were ready to defeat it. Some of the more radical sportsman vowed, "If they drag that net across or near our fishing area we will sink it with rifle fire!"

In the end, the trawler issue was a battle that lasted four years embroiling everyone in the fishing industry, fur farming, local and state wide sportsman groups, the Minnesota DNR, and our state legislature. The trawler group was led by Warroad mink rancher, George Heinen, Warroad's mayor Julius Anderson, John Pick, (brother to Uranium King Verne Pick) and two other Warroad mink farmers that operated the second trawler.

Around Warroad the controversy was bitter and it split old time friends and families. One side argued that the trawlers would destroy not only the fish habitat on Lake of the Woods, but also the existing gillnet fishermen. The other side said farmers were no longer plowing with horses, that the present fishing gear used on Lake of the Woods was obsolete, that the rough fish were needed to sustain the mink farms, and walleys should be reserved for the sportsmen.

The issue came to a climax in Warroad's municipal liquor store, Number Two, when two visitors from Roseau, whose sportsmens' clubs and farmers hated commercial fishing, ganged up on one of the local fisherman. Outnumbered he pulled out his .44 caliber pistol and fired a round of shots over their heads into the wall behind them. They never came back to Warroad and the bullet holes became quite a novelty in "Number Two".

Former State Senator Don Sinclair from Stephen was friendly towards our group. A powerful and respected member of the Senate, he side stepped the trawler issue for the first two years, while they operated under an experimental permit.

In 1963 we were ready to fight "a last ditch stand" to defeat the trawler. Dave Brewster, brother Dorrance, and myself were selected to represent the Lake of the Woods Commercial Fishermen's association at the St. Paul Legislative hearings. We knew the key to defeating the bill would be the support of our Senator, Don Sinclair, who was the Chairman of the Natural Resources Sub Committee. We must have his support if we expected to win.

It was a three-day wait until Don had a free evening to spend with us. I was the only one free that evening so the Senator and I had a pleasant dinner before discussing the fishing issue.

We spent three hours talking about Warroad's tourism and commercial fishing. My main points were the affect the trawlers were having on the Lake of the Woods and that all of the trawler's rough fish was being used for minkfeed for only two or three mink ranches. The rest of us fishermen would be forced out by the trawler gear. If that happened, fourteen licensed fishermen would be out of business along with half-a-dozen mink ranches owned by them.

The trawler bill was very simple and if it passed, its effect on the Lake of the Woods commercial fishery was a foregone conclusion. The Commissioner could issue a Commissioner's Order that the gillnets were destroying the fish population so no gillnet license would be issued. It was inevitable that would happen because the sportsmen would never allow both trawlers and gillnetters on Lake of the Woods.

But in spite of this, or probably because of it, Chuck Burrows was leaving no stone unturned to assure passage of the trawler bill. An example of his power was the offer of a timber lobbyist to help us defeat the DNR's bill. He said he had been contacted by one of his clients to help us out. We asked him, "What will your help cost us?" He said, "Nothing." We always thought our benefactor was Warroad's timber dealer, George Marvin, Sr. George supported commercial fishing feeling it did more good than harm to the lake. We never did find out because our new found friend dropped our case because the DNR informed him, "If you continue to lobby for the Lake of the Woods fishermen and against the DNR's trawler bill, your timber clients will suffer the consequence." With a wife and eight kids to feed he said, "I am sorry I cannot help you anymore, I have to feed my family."

Talking to Senator Sinclair in his office, we found he was concerned about taking away the livelihood of the commercial fishermen and their families. He also indicated that commercial fishing was not a popular political issue but the trawlers were stirring up a storm.

I agreed with him pointing out that we were there first. And that it was a case of the rich getting richer. My next meeting with him was when he came up to me in the hotel lobby, "Alvin, I want to continue our discussion about Lake of the Woods commercial fishery and how the use of ocean type trawlers will effect the industry. Meet me over at the DNR Commissioner's office at 9 a.m. tomorrow morning." I did not know what to expect but knew that Senator Sinclair was about to open up political doors that I had never imagined existed before.

The next morning when I arrived at the Commissioner's office, Senator Sinclair was waiting for me. When he introduced me to the Commissioner, I felt I was meeting a pleasant man. He was short and a little on the pudgy side. There is one thing that is still vivid in my mind, he was wearing bright red stockings.

With the DNR committed to support the trawler bill I knew I must be careful. I would follow Senator Sinclair's footsteps hoping that he would support us.

When the introductions were over Senator Sinclair said, "Commissioner, Alvin has some things to say I think you should listen to. I have another meeting to attend so will leave you two to talk it over."

I explained how all commercial gear was and should be regulated; that the department's trawler bill did not provide for mesh size control; and therefore, they would harvest immature fish before they had a chance to spawn. Another loop hole was the trawler mesh size was not regulated. That without regulating the gear the trawlers would deplete Lake of the Woods in ten to twenty years.

## Battle Over Trawling

The Commissioner listened intently, then he called Chuck Burrows into his office. When Chuck came in the Commission said, "Alvin, has made some points on the use of trawlers on Lake of the Woods. One is the mesh size used in the cod end. It is "small mesh" that will catch immature size fish that will be crushed when the cod end is hoisted up by winches. There is no way to sort out and return undersized fish or undesired fish, like walleyes, to the lake. The other problem is the head size of the trawl must be regulated."

Chuck argued that nothing should be changed, that he would regulate the type and size gear the trawlers would use. He knew and I knew that if the mesh size of the cod end was increased to three-and-a-half inches, the profitable sauger catch would be eliminated. The increased mesh size would also increase the amount of fish gilled in the cod end. My intention was to restrict the trawler's harvest with the hope they would go away, and thus us gillnetters would be able to continue fishing.

Chuck was unhappy with the turn of events and argued back and forth with the Commissioner until he stepped out of bounds and the Commissioner's mood changed and he became angry and told Chuck, "You and Alvin go back to your office where you will listen to what he has to say. I agree with him, we must regulate the trawler gear like we regulate the other gear."

When Chuck again objected to any changes in the trawler bill, the Commissioner jumped up from his desk and said, "Chuck, you go with Alvin and make those changes or I will make sure those two trawlers will never turn a wheel on Lake of the Woods again." The meeting was over and thanks to Senator Sinclair, I had won.

Returning to Chuck's office, the Director of Game and Fish was not happy, nor did he know where I was getting my clout with his boss.

He amended their bill to restrict the nets to a head rope (net opening) of 88 feet which formed a bag opening 40 feet wide and 11 feet high. The mesh size of the cod end or bag was restricted to three-an-a-half inches. The new bill also stated the trawler boats could not exceed a displacement weight of 26 tons.

At the Senate hearing our opposition was bolstered by sportsmen clubs, but the die was cast, the DNR's bill would pass. We were able to get an amendment that the trawlers would only be licensed for two years 1963 and 1964. It was a limited victory for us but would give us time for the next round in 1965.

Opposition to the use of trawlers on Lake of the Woods continued to increase in the next two years. We were no longer the only ones opposed to trawling. During the next two years the mink business was good, everybody was making money and so every box of minkfeed was in demand. Over 85% of Lake of the Woods' commercial catch, or all of its tullibee and burbot catch, was then utilized as mink feed. From 1955-68 29 million pounds of Lake of the Woods fish were utilized as minkfeed.

When the trawler vote came up again in 1965 we still opposed their use despite their continued support by the DNR. Our delegation in St. Paul continued a aggressive program to eliminate the ocean-type gear from Lake of the Woods.

Our friend, Senator Sinclair, suggested we meet with Julius Anderson and John Pick, trawler operators and supporters, to try and work out a compromise before the whole industry was toppled.

## Battle Over Trawling

Gillnetter Dave Brewster and I arranged to meet with them in the morning before the Committee's hearing. Dave and I agreed to support their bill if they included an amendment to allow 50 mesh deep gillnets instead of the 30 mesh then allowed. It was a good compromise with Senator Sinclair's promise of support. Julius Anderson agreed but John Pick would not. It was their bill so they were the only ones that could amend it.

When the committee hearing was held Chairman Senator Sinclair announced a amendment would be introduced. The room was silent. As everybody waited, not a word from Julius or John. Calling for a vote the trawler bill lost.

On looking back it was a mistake that the trawler people did not accept our compromise, instead they depended on Chuck Burrows to save them.

With no market for rough fish the trawler will never be used on Lake of the Woods again. The eventual demise of the mink ranches destroyed the market for tullibees, removing any incentive to ever harvest the rough fish with either gillnets or any other gear.

Ocean type trawlers were first tried on a experimental basis on Lake of the Woods for two years and at the end of that time the legislature passed a bill allowing their use for another two year period. At the end of that time the Trawler Bill was defeated and that type of gear was no longer used on Lake of the Woods. The picture shows "Happy" Floe dipping tullibees on the deck of their trawler. The trawler was a volume gear that caught tons of tullibees but was not accepted by the resorts, sport fishermen, or the other commercial fishermen. The battle over their use was very bitter, pitting friend against friend. Photo, Warroad Heritage Center.

# 27

## Fighting for our Lives

One battle seemed to lead to another after the use of ocean trawlers on Lake of the Woods was defeated. The political fight between the resort interests and commercial fishermen would create bitterness between Roseau, Baudette, and Warroad. Warroad fought to save commercial fishing while Roseau and Baudette used all the political clout they could muster to destroy the industry. The embattled commercial fishermen were in a political fight that would destroy them and their way of life.

Upsetting the delicate balance of fish removal with a program that encourages the game fish harvest, such as walleye pike, while neglecting to harvest the rough fish is already creating a negative effect on the walleye fishery in Lake of the Woods. In small lakes this negative effect could be offset by planting walleye fry and fingerlings but the big lake is too large to receive any benefit from restocking.

Tourism was and is promoted and subsidized by the state as the number one industry with all the politician jumping on the bandwagon. Their opinion was that commercial fishing was not compatible with tourism despite the position of the fishery research people in the Minnesota DNR. In 1970 and again in 1980, DNR research pointed out that: (1) sport fishing harvest exceeds the commercial harvest two to three times in weight and four to five times in number; (2) sport fishermen harvest a high percentage of walleye before they reach maturity contributing to small size fish by limiting the number that escape for further growth, and (3) all age classes of walleyes had very healthy populations and Lake of the Woods was Minnesota's best fishing lake.

The fact that Lake of the Woods was already producing Minnesota's finest walleye fishing did not change the hue and cry of the sport fishing community. In the 1980's they wanted it better than the best. They refused to ackowledge the fact that the commercial catch was only 15% game fish and 85% rough fish. They did not believe the DNR when they said there was plenty of walleye to maintain adequate brood stock to maintain a stable walleye population in Lake of the Woods for both the commercial and sport fishery. The lake is shallow with sandbars covered with clear blue water that is always fresh as it flows north through the Canadian White Shell area to the Winnipeg River and on up to Lake Winnipeg. This makes excellent natural spawning beds.

Walleye, saugers, and northern pike are the favorite sport fish—there are no bass, lake trout, or muskies on the Minnesota side. Twenty different species of rough fish populate Lake of the Woods each one competing with the other and the sport fish. In Lake of the Woods, the burbot is the most likely species to influence the walleye population because it is both a predator and competitor for both food and space. The tullibee is by far, the most bountiful fish in the shallow Minnesota waters. It is a plankton feeder so does not compete with the walleye for food. In fact, it is food for the walleye. However tullibee schools are so dense that they crowd out all other species, including walleye pike.

Trying to explain the complex nature of the lake, I was a willing speaker before any sport organizations that would ask me, though few wanted to ask. I would argue that even if commercial fishing was nonexistent, pressure on the walleye by Minnesota-based sport fishermen must be controlled more carefully in the future. In 1983, DNR biologist Dennis Schupp and I were part of a panel to address the Minnesota coalition of sportmen's clubs at their annual winter meeting in St. Paul. It was a hostile crowd and I was glad Dennis was there with me. Dennis believed that commercial fishing and sport fishing were compatible on Lake of the Woods. We were able to keep the lid on the meeting by answering their questions honestly.

The "abolitionists" were saying that walleye pike should be removed from restaurants although they are Minnesota wildlife products.

I stated that fish differ from big game and that the precedent has already been set to serve fish in public eating places. The dispute was an example of our conflicting values.

We soon became a favorite target of the Twin Cities sports writers. The attacks were brutal and unfair. Because my family and I were prominent in commercial fishing we received the brunt of the attack. Our opponents used all the power of the media and we were subjected to a barrage of criticism that

## 238 TIME TO FISH—TIME TO DRY NETS

became painful to me when even my family was dragged in it.

One incident I remember is when a lady cab driver picked me up at a restaurant and drove me back to my hotel. Later my room phone began ringing with coarse and uncouth voices telling me it was their turn now and send my woman companion over to their room. The story traveled through out the capitol as I made my rounds lobbying for the fisherman.

In another incident my two sons, Alan and Arthur, were accused, by Minnesota's major sport tabloid, of molesting women after organizers of a state-wide sprotsmens' group had kicked them out of their annual St. Paul meeting. It was a vicious plot designed to destroy our credibility in St. Paul and our lifetime of work on Lake of the Woods.

Using common sense and proven facts we tried to fight back by writing articles and making personal contacts with members of the legislature and sportfishing community but we were ineffective. If honesty and fair play are part of the legislative process it was not apparent to us. Representing ourselves as hard working independent decent folks, we were asking for nothing more than a chance to make a living as commercial fishermen.

In the past we were able to generate reluctant support when we testified that the mink industry was dependent on commercial fishermen and that it employed over a hundred people and generated hundreds of thousands of dollars for Roseau and Lake of the Woods counties. But due to the refusal of the DNR to transfer gillnet licenses from father to son, the numbers and the political clout of the commercial fishermen had steadily declined. All the fish caught by commercial fisherman were now being use for human food, and as usual, the consumer was ignored in this issue.

Since the end of World War II we had enjoyed the support of State Senator Sinclair from our district. A fine Senator, he was respected and was one of the most powerful and fair lawmaker in the State. After Sinclair's retirement, Senator Stumpf and Representative Jim Tunheim changed the balance of political power in our area and ignorance again ruled. We no longer had friends in the legislature. Without their help we had little or no chance to save commercial fishing. Supported by the sportsmen, the politicians and the upper level bureaucrats of the DNR argued that commercial fishing was not compatible with their vision of how to use Lake of the Woods. In the long run there was no way we could fight our own elected representatives and win in St. Paul. Not only did we have our own politicians to fight with, but distant and politically ambitious Detroit Lakes Senator Collin Peterson introduced legislation to close commercial fishing on Lake of the Woods. Our troubles mounted when a political committee calling itself "Save Our Game Fish Committee" was spearheaded by an unknown from the Fargo-Moorehead area. His name was Dick Knutson and he had lots of money and contacts. He loved to appear on TV or in the newspapers. I felt the issue counted little with Dick—being front and center was his game. Like Senator Collin Peterson, this "nobody" had found a home fighting commercial fishermen.

As the commercial fishing issue heated up in St. Paul, the few political friends we had cooled off and slammed doors in our face and avoided any contact with our delegation. We stood alone in St. Paul.

At this time I came to the difficult decision that one way or another commercial fishing on Lake of the Woods would end without more political support. Under the present DNR program no new gillnet licenses had been transferred or issued since they had they had eliminated licenses to the Northwest Angle in 1946. Since then, all gillnet licenses reverted back to the state when a license holder died. It was the cheapest and most politically correct program the DNR could come up with, though it was probably illegal. I knew that we must change that policy.

Spending as much time as I could in St. Paul, my efforts were rewarded when DNR Commissioner Joe Alexander decided to call for a commission of four people, one fisherman, one resort owner, one sportsman, and one fish buyer to meet in St. Paul to try and work out a compromise plan that would satisfy everybody.

The meeting was chaired by Mr. Hanson from the DNR. Alexander appointed John Beckle from Sportsman's Lodge in Baudette to represent Minnesota's resorts. John's program was, "If the commercial harvest of walleye pike is to continue it should be done with hooks instead of nets." One evening in the hotel, John was discouraged after a hard day of lobbying. He turned to me and said, "Alvin, I am going to go to a health spa and loose thirty pounds, quit smoking, drinking and sex so I can live long enough to get you off the lake!"

Alexander's second appointment to the commission was Dick Knutson as representative of the organized, down-state sportsmen organizations. Abrasive and formidable, he was not liked by anybody, even the organizations that paid him. How he got into the Lake of the Woods politics, nobody

## Fighting for our Lives

seemed to know. It appeared he was a paid lobbyist and was certainly generating a lot of money. He used the Ducks Unlimited approach to fund raising and at his numerous parties he usually took in more money in one night then some of us commercial fishermen made in one year. Where did all that money go? It has still never been accounted for.

To me there was a difference between Dick Knutson and John Beckle. John and I had something in common—we did care about Lake of the Woods. On the other hand, Dick Knutson loved the publicity, the money, and the press coverage that the issue was generating. I felt Dick could care less about Lake of the Woods or its future.

The third member was Loren Morey. He was a businessman, steady and knowledgeable. His father had bought the old Selvog Fishery in the 60's and Loren had just built a new fishery building in Warroad. He knew all there was to know about the fish business. A good man to sit beside you.

The fourth member was myself. I knew what I wanted; the transfer of gillnet licenses. It seemed like an impossible dream but without it we had little or no leverage. I decided to fight to the end for it.

The meeting started in the morning and we haggled until lunch break without agreeing on anything. Mr. Hanson from the DNR did a good job of keeping the meeting on a somewhat level playing ground. After lunch we convened again and battled until we took a three o'clock break. Loren and I held our ground on the license transfer. Looking for a Coke machine, Loren met the Commissioner down a hallway. The Commissioner told Loren, "Hold your ground, because Governor Quie phoned me and said he would veto any bill that discriminated against a group of legitimate businessmen."

Toward evening we were all tired out from arguing for the past eight hours. I knew that John and Dick felt little compassion for the embattled commercial fishermen so I decided to give it my best shot. I became angry and zeroed in on John, "John, I know plenty about the tourist business, things that can make your business more difficult than it already is and if you are going to take the commercial fisherman down I am going to take you with us. I do not know how much you are worth, but I think I can match you dollar-for-dollar and I will spend every penny I have fighting you. John, we are going down together." That outburst, along with agreeing to close certain areas to gillnets was the basis for a compromise agreement allowing the transfer of gillnet license for the first time in thirty-five years.

Mr. Hanson said a Commissioner's Order would be issued allowing the transfer to qualified applicants. The University of Minnesota would conduct a study and the agreement was to be reviewed in two years when another meeting would be held. It was a dream come true—my two sons, Alan and Arthur, would both have a gillnet license. They would become the fourth generation of my family to commercially fish Lake of the Woods. I transferred my license to Alan and Arthur bought "Two Gun" Brewster's outfit.

After the transfer of gillnet licenses, our agreement with Commissioner Alexander called for a two year cooling off period and for the University of Minnesota to conduct a more thorough study of the fishery.

# 28

# From Fishing to Gambling Casinos

After the agreement, it did not take long for the anti-commercial fishing groups to realize that the rules of the game had changed. They became aware that the new license holders would perpetuate commercial fishing for a number of years. The very next year State Senator Collin Peterson reneged on his word, ignored the scientific research, and introduced a bill to eliminate commercial fishing on Lake of the Woods and Rainy Lake. Peterson is now a U.S. Representative in Washington cutting deals.

We were astounded to hear of the Senator's, the sportsmens', and the DNR's double cross. We felt the next two years would be trouble free, allowing us to concentrate on the difficult task of making a living as commercial fishermen on Lake of the Woods. At an emergency session, the Lake of the Woods Commercial Fishermen's Association selected a delegation to attend the Senate hearing on Senator Peterson's bill.

Meeting with Senator Peterson in his Senate office, his demeanor was apologetic, but he obviously was more concerned about trying to get U.S. Representative Arlan Stangeland's job than he was in listening to common sense and scientific research. The misery he was putting us through was just political hay for his career as a politician. He knew that if he was to challenge Stangeland he needed the name recognition that his anti-commercial fishing bill would generate. He told us that he agreed with the DNR fishery research that there was nothing wrong with the fish population on Lake of the Woods, but he said that there was a public perception of a problem so that's why he had to remove commercial fishing.

The Senate Committee did not vote his bill down. I addressed the committee and stated that the commercial fishermen were getting a raw deal and that the new bill was not what we had agreed on only one year before. I indicated there was no future for our industry when our own government's commitments would not be honored by the State's legislative bodies and the DNR. After a series of meetings with the Chairman of the Natural Resource Committee Gene Merriam and Senators Collin Peterson, Bob Lessard, Keith Langseth, Charles Berg, and others, I came to the conclusion that none of them would support us, however most of them expressed concern about destroying the livelihood of so many people and seemed willing to work out a financial program to assist in relocating families. I eventually had to indicate the commercial fishermen would look at a state buy-out program, if one could be agreed on. For this phase of the agreement, my two sons Alan and Arthur spent most of the winter in St. Paul lobbying for a fair and just amount of money for the fishermen.

## From Fishing to Gambling Casinos 245

We thought we had a "marker" on Minnesota's new Governor, Rudy Perpich, because we had supported his campaign for governor with a $500 donation. While Perpich was in International Falls attending a political rally, Representative Irv Anderson had arranged a meeting with candidate Perpich with fish buyer Jim McCarthy, my son Arthur, and myself at a vacant motel room at the Holiday Inn. Candidate Perpich was interested in commercial fishing and indicated he enjoyed eating fish and that he had a concern of who would supply the market if commercial fishing was voted out. He said that while working in Europe, fish was a major food item. He asked intelligent questions like: "What does Joe Alexander, DNR Commissioner, think about it? What will the commercial fishermen do if they lose their license? How will Warroad be affected if the industry dies?" It was a serious meeting and the future Governor patted Arthur and me on the shoulder and said, "You have a friend here."

Encouraged by our visit with candidate Perpich, we decided to donate to his campaign. Jim McCarthy said he would contact the Perpich committee and give them our check. A few days later, when I checked with him he said, "When I contacted the local campaign committee I was told to make the check out to the Minnesota Right To Life Committee because all of their funds were going to Candidate Perpich." He did that and our $500 was lost in the world of politics. The only thing we gained was experience, and thought we would not be so naive next time.

Vice Chairman of the Natural Resources Committee in the House, Dave Battaglia, became another enemy because he was resentful that a number of commercial fishermen from Two Harbors had lost their Lake Superior commercial fishing licenses. Battaglia's program was simple, he said, "The commercial fishermen in my district did not receive compensation so therefore, the Lake of the Woods commercial fishermen should receive none."

He was a heavyset man with a round face that never smiled. His English had a sort of a guttural accent. He ruled the roost on the Natural Resources Committee and tried to dominate the Minnesota DFL members. Most of them seemed frightened of him. He talked about the noble goals of the House, but forgot to practice them. He turned out to be our worst enemy.

I remember a hearing on Lake of the Woods commercial fishing chaired by Battaglia that used up the morning with unrelated speeches. The commercial fishing delegation, waited and waited, until close to noon before we were called. When he called my name, I walked to the podium, and began my presentation with my name and the organization I represented. That was as far as I got, Chairman Battaglia's gavel banged the table, and he said, "Meeting adjourned." I never had a chance to say one word. It was democracy in action, "Battaglia style." As the weeks passed nothing improved our relationship with him.

The Senate and House's bills to eliminate commercial fishing were not originally supported by the DNR fishery researchers, but the higher-up DNR people agreed to go along with it when the Legislature included a permanent $2.50 surcharge on all sportfishing licenses in return for the DNR's support to eliminate the commercial fishing. This made getting rid of commercial fishing a financial windfall for the DNR that the bureaucrats couldn't resist. The DNR "researchers" then authored the wording to eliminate the commercial fishermen by a forced buy-out of their licenses based on a fabricated quota.

Our DNR contact was with the DNR's new director of Game and Fish, Dick Hassinger. He was a "grinning jackass" that laughed at us when we tossed out our first buy-out amount that was taken from the 1970 DNR study on the lake. He indicated to us that as far as his office was concerned, we would get nothing. Several times he told us that the sportsmen of Minnesota pay his salary and he does what they tell him to do.

After weeks of haggling the, commercial fishermen agreed on a $70,000 buy-out plan. The DNR authored it such that no walleyes could be harvested by commercial fishermen and no gillnets could be used. The buy-out amount was based on so much per pound of walleye pike that the average fishermen would catch with their annual walleye harvest. But then to limit the amount of buy-out that we would get, the DNR wrote in that that quota would diminish to zero in eight years. We would be given nothing for the loss of the ability to catch any other fish so we got nothing for 85% of our traditional catch. Then they threw in a discount factor which we knew nothing about, but which further reduced our buy-out by 25%. Still politically naive and knowing nothing about formal economics and law, we thought we had no choice but to accept the discount rate. One year after that, all the commercial fisherman took the buyout except my son Arthur.

Contrary to common knowledge a commercial fishing license can still be issued by the DNR with the provision only that no gillnets are used and that no walleyes are harvested. But without walleyes and gillnets, there is no longer an economic incentive for anyone to fish.

Things are different now—the big lake is looked at as a recreation body of water, something that is only useful to play on. As long as fishing is good the boats will flock in—as the quality of fishing declines so will the sport fishermen. They will find other lakes to fish and enjoy boating.

On the other hand the commercial fishermen loved the lake. It was our bread and butter. We stayed with it through lean years and through good years. The Lake of the Woods was home and livelihood to us for four generations.

I had my chance to take a whack or two at Collin Peterson a few days before his election to Congress in 1992. I received a phone call from a person that said he was Peterson's campaign manager. He did not say how he knew me nor why he thought I could help him. After identifying himself he asked me, "Do you know a person by the name of Dick Knutson?" I said I did. "Then you are my man". He said that a newspaper reporter was publishing a scandalous story in a tabloid about Peterson. His manager thought the story could destroy his chance of winning the election. "Why is that?", I said.

"Because the story is about a party at a sportsmen's resort in the Northwest Angle that Peterson had hosted for some CPAs," the manager indicated. He further indicted that sex was involved and Peterson's scandalous behavior was "sleazy" politics. The manager said that with no time to fight back, the story might cause Peterson to lose the election. He said a reporter would be phoning me in a few minutes to see if I would confirm the story.

I told him I did not like sleazy stories about anyone but he was talking to the wrong person because I was not going to vote for Peterson. It was my understanding that State Senator Leroy Stumpf had suggested he call me.

In a few minutes the phone rang again and it was the newspaper reporter looking for confirmation for this story. I was honest when I told him I had not heard about that party and suggested that he drive up to Warroad and investigate the story out at the resort where it happened. I also informed him that he could not use my name in his story. I suggested that he phone the Trueman Resort at Baudette and that Mike Trueman might be able to shed some light on his story.

In the morning, Peterson's manager phoned me and said the newspaper story had been pulled. Telling the story to a friend of mine from the Angle after the election, I was surprised when he said, "Yes, I heard about that party!"

What bothers me today is that if I had known about the story when the newspaper reporter phoned me, would I have reacted by confirming it? If I had, could it have changed the outcome of the election? Would I, or should I have sought political revenge on an ignoble politician who destroyed my family's industry and lifestyle?

Just a couple of years ago I attended the grand opening of the new Red Lake Indian tribe's gambling casino in Warroad. They had bought and renovated the Morey Fish House, where Lake of the Woods commercial fishermen had sold their fish for close to a hundred years, into their casino. Nearly everyone in northern Minnesota and North Dakota had bought their fish at Morey's Fish House—now it was a casino. Congressman Peterson and State Representative Tunheim were the speakers for the grand opening honoring the new casino. Listening to their warm words of praise and encouragement I thought, "What a turnabout! They now support and encourage casino gambling as a compatible and useful tool in the tourist development of Lake of the Woods in place of a commercial fishery that produced food for people that enjoyed eating fish but for one reason or another were unable to catch them!"

The Native Americans never altered or changed the lake in hundreds of years because they were "native" to it. The lake did not began to change until the late 1800's when the dam was built in Kenora and the big fishery started. But even those changes on the lake had little effect on the long term health of the resource. However, in just the last twenty-five years, increased tourist traffic and sportfishing usage have had a lasting and perhaps devastating effect on the lake, the shoreline, and on the culture of those that depend on it for a living.

# 29

## Reeling Them In

Written by Arthur Johnston. Originally published in the *National Fisherman*.

It's a beautiful day to go fishing. The wind is low. It's above freezing. Some light snow in the air. I get to my fishery and find that there are already three customers waiting to buy fish from me. The conversation is typical. But today is the last day I'll have it:

"Do you have any walleyes for sale?"

"Nope."

"Will you have any for sale later?"

"Nope. All the walleyes I can catch have been sold long ago. You had to put in an order at least two weeks ahead of time. But today is the last day."

"Do you have any northerns?"

"No. But come back later. When I get off the lake in about four hours there's a possibility that I will have some extra."

"Do you have any saugers or perch or anything?"

"All I've got are tullibees and suckers. But they're real cheap."

"I wouldn't take those fish it you gave them to me. Where else can I get walleyes?"

"I'm the last fisherman here. And I'm the last walleye fisherman in the States."

"What happened to all the fishermen that used to be around here."

"Well, the fish are in the lake. If you want to find out what happened to all our fisherman go talk to your local friendly politicians. If you want to buy any fish, go to Canada."

My helper, John LaChappelle, and I load up my boat with fish boxes and start up my 19-foot outboard. Unlike most of the outboards that I have had, the new oil injection V-4 Johnson starts right up in spite of the freezing weather. We head out to the lake to get my fish for the day and to pull my nets— for the last time.

It's a beautiful day. Doesn't seem like the normal last day of fishing on the last day of October. There is no ice on the water and it's not blizzarding. I would almost call it a pleasant day if I didn't know that this would be the last time I would be doing this.

There are no other boats on the lake. In fact, there are no other boats even left in the water in the Warroad River Harbor. Except for a couple little kickers that some diehard bluebill hunters might be using. It's rare to see a sport boat (or the more commonly referred to names of "weekend warriors," "hookers," or "pukers") on the open lake after Labor Day weekend. Since all the other commercial fisherman quit last year, to see any boat at all out in the lake at this time of year is as rare as seeing a Sabine's Gull. It's kind of lonely.

We go several miles east of Warroad, to the best walleye and northern spot on Lake of the Woods. Several more miles and I would be where my great uncle drown many years ago. We get to the net buoy and John quickly has the net up. We start picking the fish. We are wearing rubber gloves for protection from the freezing water and wind, but our hands are still cold.

Today's catch is what I expected. Too many walleyes and too few northerns. 100 more pounds of walleyes and I fill up my quota. I get that 100 pounds in the first 400 feet of net.

This whole year has been atypical. Normally I would be fishing all my legally allowed 3,000 feet of gillnets, but now I've only got 1,000 feet of net out. Fishing such a small amount of gear means it will be another easy day. If I had been fishing all my gear I would have filled up the walleye quota that the politicians had put on me in only one month. The biggest abnormality of the year is that I have been trying not to catch them. Nearly all my fishing life I've spent trying to catch walleyes. They're the money fish. But this year I've tried every trick of the trade not to catch walleye. Maybe old habits die hard. No matter what I do I keep catching too many walleyes.

So I return the excess walleyes to the lake. Nearly all of them are alive in my gillnets and the only damage to them is occasional scales pulled off in getting them out of the net. At this time of year, the gillnet does less damage to walleye than a sportsman's hook does.

It seems silly to pick a fish just to have to throw it back and I am glad that there are fewer walleyes here then there's been most of the month. It's been a hard year in the sense that I've had to throw so much money away. Every walleye I've thrown back is throwing away $4. I've thrown back thousands of them—and thousands and thousands of dollars.

Politics is more than silly, it's disgusting. As one of the fishery scientists once told me, "Back in the feudal days, the resources were divvied up according to the whims of the kings and nobleman. But now it's different. Now the people holding political power divvy it up according to their whims."

There's no quota on northerns. They are the second money fish so that is what I've been trying to catch. There are some northerns in the net, but not as many as there are walleyes. This year the fall northern run didn't come in as heavy as I hoped. I remember falls when I had so many northerns that I had to make two trips with my boat to haul them all.

Compared to walleyes, northerns are a real pain in the neck. They are hard to untangle from a gillnet, they are hard to hold on to, and my hands tire out quickly in picking them. But they are good money. The whole reason that I've delayed filling my walleye quota is that I was hoping to cash in on the fall northern run. Oh, I've done all right—a lot better then if I'd taken the money that the State tried to buy me out with. But still, I'll never fill up the customer's orders with northerns this year.

Luckily, the tullibee fall run hasn't started. The couple boxes a day that I get is all that I can handle. It used to be that you could make a bit of money on tullibees when Morey's Fishery was open. They would do all the dressing and all you would have to do is haul the tullibees there. But you had to haul them by the boat load to make money. Morey's Fishery is closed this year. I am the only fisherman and they weren't going to stay open just for me. Consequently, I've got to do all the tullibee dressing and transportation myself. More then three or four boxes and I am swamped and the wholesale price is so low that I can't afford to hire someone to dress them. And when tullibees come they come by the ton. Many times this year I've had to move my nets to avoid getting overrun by tullibees.

Another fish I would like to avoid but never can are suckers. They are worth less than tullibees and about 1% the price of walleyes. Unfortunately, it is next to impossible to avoid suckers and next to impossible to sell them. They are everywhere in the lake. The only way I avoid them is to float my nets off the bottom. One foot off the bottom and I won't get any suckers. More than one foot and I usually don't get anything else either, so I just suffer by picking the suckers.

There are lots of burbot here. Fortunately, gillnet don't catch too many of them. We can tell that there are a lot of them here because they swallow the walleyes and tullibees that are caught in the net, but then regurgitate the fish just before we can grab them from the boat. The number of fish that are scaled or half-digested is a better indication of the number of burbot then is the actual amount that we catch. Burbot are too smart to get caught. Maybe that is why some people call them "lawyers." I never could figure out who was named after who.

Though most of the burbot get away on their own, we usually still get a couple boxes; but those I do get, I just throw back anyway. I haven't sold a burbot for at least three years, since most of the mink farms went out of business. Two years ago I brought some burbot into the fishery that a guy had ordered. He never came to pick them up. Maybe he thought the dime a pound that I was charging was too much.

The politicians, the DNR, and the sports kept telling us, "We don't want to put you out of business. We just want you to stop catching walleyes. There are lots of fish out there you can make money at. You just aren't trying hard enough to sell those other fish."

Well, maybe they are right. Maybe we could make a living without walleyes—I was willing to give it a try, and there are sure plenty of fish in the lake. If I wanted to be a fisherman, I had no choice but to give it a try. The politicians only banned gillnets and catching walleye. We could still use trapnets and catch northerns, perch, and saugers. None of the other fisherman were willing to give it a try, but I went to Green Bay on Lake Michigan and bought some perch nets and used my father's license to experiment with them. And they worked! They not only caught lots of perch, but also saugers; and both of these had prices comparable to walleyes. It looked like I had found a way to keep fishing and still be within the limits of the new law!...

But I underestimated the DNR's antagonism toward commercial fishing. As soon as the DNR figured I was serious about fishing for perch and saugers with trapnets, they took it upon themselves to expand the walleye ban, by Commissioner's Order, to all fish except tullibees, suckers, and burbot. Right. Sure. The DNR isn't trying to put us out of business; we can still make a living catching burbot and suckers and tullibees.

Well, maybe we can still make a living—just have the government build a fish processing plant, then have the government buy fishing gear, then have the government pay me to catch the fish, then have the government pay someone to take the finished product. No problem. But no thanks, I'll go someplace else and make an honest living. But don't worry though. There will always be someone to help out the government. If nothing else, they can always go to the local bars and find some sports who

## Reeling Them In

are willing to donate their time to the worthy cause of removing the scourge of rough fish from the lake.

John and I finish picking the fish. We dress the northerns and suckers on the boat and give the Herring Gulls one last feast. The tullibees are too hard to dress on the boat and the DNR doesn't allow us to fillet the walleyes on the lake.

John LaChappelle was the manager at Morey's Fishery for forty years. He is the hardest working man that I know. He used to be up before 6 am to get us fishermen ice, and then he would frequently be working at dressing tullibees till late in the night. John probably knows more about Lake of the Woods and the fishermen than anyone one else.

John's been helping me out this year since Morey's isn't open anymore. He had a hard time keeping away from any fishing activity. First he just came down to help me fillet and get in on some fishery talk that we always shared before. But after my nephew who was my helper started back to high school, John also started coming out on the lake with me. Before this year he hardly ever went out with any of the fishermen, because he was always too busy managing Morey's. But this year he's got in on the fish catching end of the fishing industry.

As manager of Morey's Fishery, John was a major character in the Lake of the Woods fishing industry from it's heyday up to last year when most of the industry was shut down.

It's fitting that John is here with me helping pull the last nets on the last day of fishing. We never talk much. But today there is even less talk. We both know each other's thoughts—this is the last day. What we've both done all our lives will soon be done for the last time.

## 258  TIME TO FISH—TIME TO DRY NETS

After we finish dressing the fish (or putting clothes on these fish as John would say) we go to the upwind end of the net, pull the buoy, anchor and then start pulling the net. Every thing goes smoothly.

I bought this old 19-foot, 1961 fiberglass Pipestone from "Two Gun" Brewster. Several years ago I rebuilt it—a clear Doug Fir 2 X 6 for the keel, local White Cedar for the ribs, two 3/4 inch pieces of marine plywood for the transom, a new plywood floor, and a forward bulkhead to stiffen the bow were securely glassed to the original Pipestone glass hull.

This boat is pure function. Everything has its place. There is nothing fancy or frivolous on it. The bow and stern are open to enable us to lift and pull nets in the most efficient manner which depends on the weather. The outboard controls are in the middle. There are no seats unless we sit on fish boxes. There is no room to put on a windshield so we are always exposed to the weather. Oilers are necessaryto keep the bow spray off of us on all but the calmest days. Everything is done by hand. No net lifters. We don't even have an electronic depth gauge or fish finder—lead lines are more dependable, and anyway, there are so many fish, why bother with "finding" them. No marine bands or LORAN can stand up to the constant pounding, so they're not on my boat.

The constant exposure makes this boat sometimes uncomfortable; but it's seen 14-foot waves that 60 mph winds have blown from Big Island, and I wouldn't trade it for anything. The new V-4 Johnson has made it very mechanically dependable, and it carries 2,000 pounds of fish in a heavy sea. As far as I am concerned, it's the most seaworthy

### Reeling Them In 259

and dependable boat on the Lake. But, like me, it will soon have nothing to do and what it was made for will be gone.

The net is pulled. We head back to Warroad. There are more cars around the fishery than when we left. John and I fillet up the walleyes and some of the northerns. The last walleye and then the last northern is sold. Most of the cars leave without getting any fish. There are no more fish for sale.

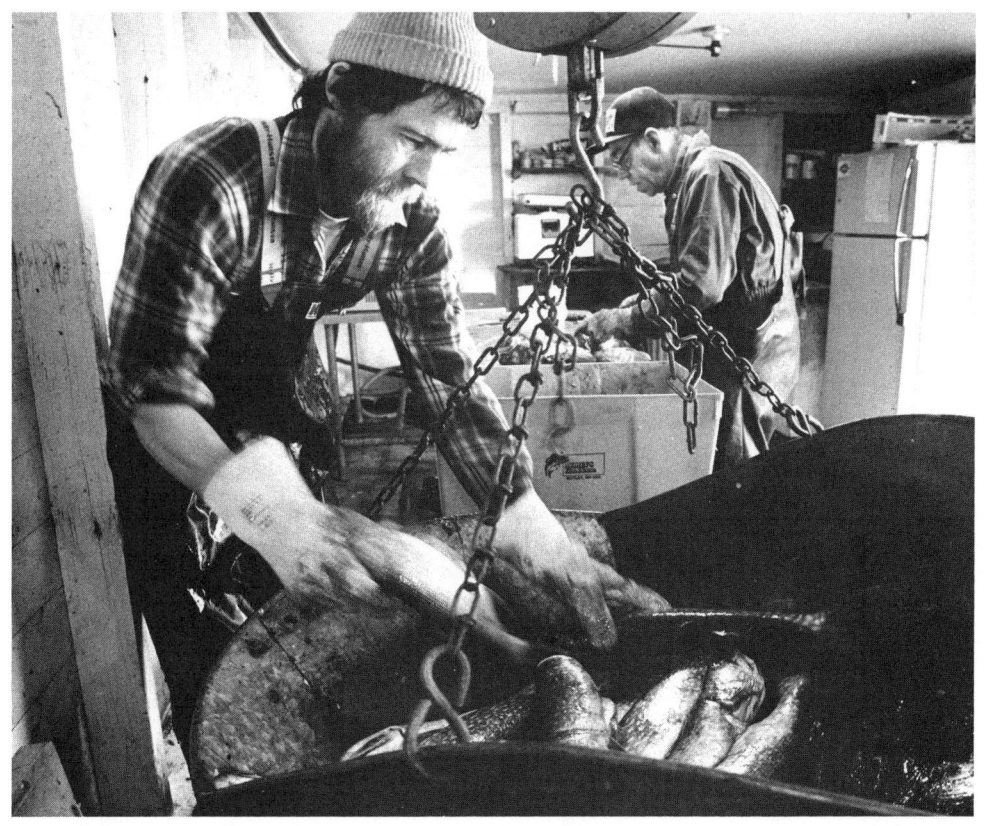

Art Johnston and John LaChappelle cleaning fish at the Lake of the Woods Fishery, across from the fire hall and about 200' from where the old Booth Fishery was located. Photo ©1985 Star Tribune, Mpls-St.Paul.

Photo ©1985 Star Tribune, Mpls-St.Paul.